ENGLISH SMALL THEORY

ARVIND & GAJANAND

ISBN 979-888530198-5

we dedicated this book to Author Nitin Punjabi .

Contents

CHAPTER ONE

The Last Lesson

About the writer :

Alphonse Daudet was a French novelist and a short-story writer and has more than three dozen works of literature to his credit. He is considered to be one of the most iconic names of French Literature. He portrayed human emotions in a very realistic manner.

I started for school very late that morning and was in great dread of a scolding, especially because M. Hamel had said that he would question us on participles, and I did not know the first word about them. For a moment I thought of running away and spending the day out of doors. It was so warm, so bright! The birds were chirping at the edge of the woods; and in the open field back of the sawmill the Prussian soldiers were drilling. It was all much more tempting than the rule for participles, but I had the strength to resist, and hurried off to school.

When I passed the town hall there was a crowd infront of the bulletin-board. For the last two years all our bad news had come from there — the lost battles, the draft, the orders of the commanding officer — and I thought to myself, without stopping, ""What can be the matter now?"

Then, as I hurried by as fast as I could go, the blacksmith, Wachter, who was there, with his apprentice, reading the bulletin, called after me, "Don't go so fast, bub; you ll get to your school in plenty of time!"

I thought he was making fun of me, and reached M. Hamel's little garden all out of breath.

Usually, when school began, there was a great bustle, which could be heard out in the street, the opening and closing of desks, lessons repeated in unison, very loud, with our hands over our ears to understand better, and the teacher's great ruler rapping on the table. But now it was all so still! I had counted on the commotion to get to my desk without being seen; but, of course, that day everything had to be as quiet as Sunday morning.

Through the window I saw my classmates, already in their places, and M. Hamel walking up and down with his terrible iron ruler under his arm. I had to open the door and go in before everybody. You can imagine how I blushed and how frightened I was.

But nothing happened. M. Hamel saw me and said very kindly, "Go to your place quickly, little Franz. We were beginning without you."

I jumped over the bench and sat down at my desk. Not till then, when I had got a little over my fright, did I see that our teacher had on his beautiful green coat, his frilled shirt, and the little black silk cap, all embroidered, that he never wore except on inspection and prize days. Besides, the whole school seemed so strange and solemn. But the thing that surprised me most was to see, on the back benches that were always empty, the village people sitting quietly like ourselves; old Hauser, with his three-cornered hat, the former mayor, the former postmaster, and several others besides. Everybody looked sad; and Hauser had brought an old primer, thumbed at the edges, and he held it open on his knees with his great spectacles lying across the pages.

While I was wondering about it all, M. Hamel mounted his chair, and, in the same grave and gentle tone which he had used to me, said, "My children, this is the last lesson I shall give you. The order has come from Berlin to teach only German in the schools of Alsace and Lorraine. The new master comes tomorrow. This is your last French lesson. I want you to be very attentive."

What a thunderclap these words were to me!

Oh, the wretches; that was what they had put up at the town-hall!

My last French lesson! Why, I hardly knew how to write! I should never learn anymore! I must stop there, then! Oh, how sorry I was for not learning my lessons, for seeking birds' eggs, or going sliding on the Saar! My books, that had seemed such a nuisance a while ago, so heavy to carry, my grammar, and my history of the saints, were old friends now that I couldn't give up. And M. Hamel, too; the idea that he was going away, that I should never see him again, made me forget all about his ruler and how cranky he was.

Poor man! It was in honour of this last lesson that he had put on his fine Sunday clothes, and now I understood why the old men of the village were sitting there in the back of the room. It was because they were sorry, too, that they had not gone to school more. It was their way of thanking our master for his forty years of faithful service and of showing their respect for the country that was theirs no more.

While I was thinking of all this, [heard my name called. It was my turn to recite. What would I not have given to be able to say that dreadful rule for the participle all through, very loud and clear, and without one mistake? But I got mixed up on the first words and stood there, holding on to my desk, my heart beating, and not daring to look up.

I heard M. Hamel say to me, "I won't scold you, little Franz; you must feel bad enough. See how it is! Every day we have said to ourselves, 'Bah! I've plenty of time. I' ll learn it tomorrow.' And now you see where we' ve come out. Ah, that's the great trouble with Alsace; she puts off learning till tomorrow. Now those fellows out there will have the right to say to you, "How is it; you pretend to be Frenchmen, and yet you can neither speak nor write your own language?' But you are not the worst, poor little Franz. We've all a great deal to reproach ourselves with."

"Your parents were not anxious enough to have you learn. They preferred to put you to work on a farm or at the mills, so as to have a little more money. And I? I've been to blame also. Have not often sent you to water my flowers instead of learning your lessons? And when I wanted to go fishing, did I not just give you a holiday?"

Then, from one thing to another, M. Hamel went on to talk of the French language, saying that it was the most beautiful language in the world — the clearest, the most logical; that we must guard it among us and never forget it, because when people are enslaved, as long as they hold fast to their language it is as if they had the key to their prison. Then he opened a grammar and read us our lesson. I was amazed to see how well I understood it. All he said seemed so easy, so easy! I think, too, that I had never listened so carefully, and that he had never explained everything with so much patience. It seemed almost as if the poor man wanted to give us all he knew before going away, and to put it all into our heads at one stroke.

After the grammar, we had a lesson in writing. That day M.Hamel had new copies for us, written in a beautiful round hand— France, Alsace, France, Alsace. They looked like little flags floating everywhere in the school-room, hung from the rod at the top of our desks. You ought to have seen how everyone set to work, and how quiet it was! The only sound was the scratching of the pens over the paper. Once some beetles flew in; but nobody paid any attention to them, not even the littlest ones, who worked right on tracing their fish-hooks, as if that was French, too. On the roof the pigeons cooed very low, and I thought to myself, "Will they make them sing in German, even the pigeons?"'

Whenever I looked up from my writing I saw M. Hamel sitting motionless in his chair and gazing first at one thing, then at another, as if he wanted to fix in his mind just how everything looked in that little school-room. Fancy! For forty years he had been there in the same place, with his garden outside the window and his class in front of him, just like that. Only the desks and benches had been worn smooth; the walnut-trees in the garden were taller, and the hop vine that he had planted himself twined about the windows to the roof. How it must have broken his heart to leave it all, poor man; to hear his sister moving about in the room above, packing their trunks! For they must leave the country next day.

But he had the courage to hear every lesson to the very last. After the writing, we had a lesson in history, and then the babies chanted their ba, be bi, bo. Down there at the back of the room old Hauser had put on his spectacles and, holding his primer in both hands, spelled the letters with them. You could see that he, too, was crying; his voice trembled with emotion, and it was so funny to hear him that we all wanted to laugh and cry. Ah, how well I remember it, that last lesson!

All at once the church-clock struck twelve. Then the Angelus. At the same moment the trumpets of the Prussians, returning from drill, sounded under our windows. M. Hamel stood up, very pale, in his chair. I never saw him look so tall.

"My friends," said he, "I—I—" But something choked him. He could not go on.

Then he turned to the blackboard, took a piece of chalk, and, bearing on with all his might, he wrote as large as he could —

"Vive La France!"

Then he stopped and leaned his head against the wall, and, without a word, he made a gesture to us with his hand —

'School is dismissed —you may go."

CHAPTER TWO

Lost Spring

Sometimes I find a rupee in the garbage'.

"Why do you do this?" I ask Saheb whom I encounter every morning scrounging for gold in the garbage dumps of my neighbourhood. Saheb left his home long ago. Set amidst the green fields of Dhaka, his home is not even a distant memory. There were many storms that swept away their fields and homes, his mother tells him. That's why they left, looking for gold in the big city where he now lives.

"I have nothing else to do," he mutters, looking away.

"Go to school," I say glibly, realising immediately how hollow the advice must sound.

"There is no school in my neighbourhood, when they build one, I will go,"

"If I start a school, will you come?" I ask, half-joking.

"Yes," he says, smiling broadly.

A few days later I see him running up to me. "Is your school ready?"

"It takes longer to build a school," I say, embarrassed at having made a promise that was not meant. But promises like mine abound in every corner of his bleak world.

After months of knowing him, I ask him his name. "Saheb-e-Alam," he announces, He does not know what it means. If he knew its meaning - lord of the universe - he would have a hard time believing it. Unaware of what his name represents, he roams the streets with his friends, an army of barefoot boys who appear like the morning birds and disappear at noon. Over the months, I have come to recognise each of them.

"Why aren't you wearing chappals?" I ask one.

"My mother did not bring them down from the shelf," he answers simply.

"Even if she did he will throw them off," adds another who is wearing shoes that do not match. When I comment on it, he shuffles his feet and says nothing. "I want shoes," says a third boy who has never owned a pair all his life. Travelling across the country I have seen children walking barefoot, in cities, on village roads. It is not lack of money but a tradition to stay barefoot, is one explanation. I wonder if this is only an excuse to explain away a perpetual state of poverty.

I remember a story a man from Udipi once told me. As a young boy he would go to school past an old temple, where his father was a priest. He would stop briefly at the temple and pray for a pair of shoes. Thirty years later I visited his town and the temple, which was now drowned in an air of desolation. In the backyard, where lived the new priest, there were red and white plastic chairs. A young boy dressed in a grey uniform, wearing socks and shoes, arrived panting and threw his school bag on a folding bed. Looking at the boy, I remembered the prayer another boy had made to the goddess when he had finally got a pair of shoes, "Let me never lose them." The goddess had granted his prayer. Young boys like the son of the priest now wore shoes. But many others like the ragpickers in my neighbourhood remain shoeless.

My acquaintance with the barefoot rag pickers leads me to Seemapuri, a place on the periphery of Delhi yet miles away from it, metaphorically. Those who live here are squatters who came from Bangladesh back in 1971. Saheb's family is among them. Seemapuri was then a wilderness. It still is, but it is no longer empty. In structures of mud, with roofs of tin and tarpaulin, devoid of sewage, drainage or running water, live 10,000 rag pickers. They have lived here for more than thirty years without an identity, without permits but with ration cards that get their names on voters' lists and enable them to buy grain. Food is more important for survival than an identity. "If at the end of the day we can feed our families and go to bed without an aching stomach, we would rather live here than in the fields that gave us no grain," say a group of women in tattered saris when I ask them why they left their beautiful land of green fields and rivers. Wherever they find food, they pitch their tents that become transit homes. Children grow up in them, becoming partners in survival. And survival in Seemapuri means rag-picking. Through the years, it has acquired the proportions of a fine art. Garbage to them is gold. It is their daily bread, a roof over their heads, even if it is a leaking roof. But for a child it is even more.

"I sometimes find a rupee, even a ten-rupee note," Saheb says, his eyes lighting up. When you can find a silver coin in a heap of garbage, you don't stop scrounging, for there is hope of finding more. It seems that for children, garbage has a meaning different from what it means to their parents. For the children it is wrapped in wonder, for the elders it is a means of survival.

One winter morning I see Saheb standing by the fenced gate of the neighbourhood club, watching two young men dressed in white, playing tennis. "I like the game," he hums; content to watch it standing behind the fence. "I go inside when no one is around," he admits "The gatekeeper lets me use the swing."

Saheb too is wearing tennis shoes that look strange over his discoloured shirt and shorts, "Someone gave them to me," he says in the manner of an explanation. The fact that they are discarded shoes of some rich boy, who perhaps refused to wear them because of a hole in one of them, does not bother him. For one who has walked barefoot, even shoes with a hole is a dream come true. But the game he is watching so intently is out of his reach.

This morning, Saheb is on his way to the milk booth. In his hand is a steel canister, "I now work in a tea stall down the road," he says, pointing in the distance, "I am paid 800 rupees and all my meals". Does he like the job? I ask. His face, I see, has lost the carefree look. The steel canister seems heavier than the plastic bag he would carry so lightly over his shoulder. The bag was his. The canister belongs to the man who owns the tea shop, Saheb is no longer his own master.

"I want to drive a car."

Mukesh insists on being his own master, "I will be a motor mechanic," he announces.

"Do you know anything about cars?" I ask.

"I will learn to drive a car," he answers, looking straight into my eyes. His dream looms like a mirage admidst the dust of streets that fill his town Firozabad, famous for its bangles. Every other family in Firozabad is engaged in making bangles. It is the centre of India's glass-blowing industry where families have spent generations working around furnaces, welding glass, making bangles for all the women in the land it seems.

Mukesh's family is among them. None of them knows that it is illegal for children like him to work in the glass furnaces with high temperatures, in dingy cells without air and light; that the law, if enforced, could get him and all those 20,000 children out of the hot furnaces where they slog their daylight hours, often losing the brightness of their eyes. Mukesh's eyes beam as he volunteers to take me home, which he proudly says is being rebuilt. We walk down stinking lanes choked with garbage, past homes that remain hovels with crumbling walls, wobbly doors, no windows, crowded with families of humans and animals coexisting in a primeval state. He stops at the door of one such house, bangs a wobbly iron door with his foot, and pushes it open we enter a half-built shack. In one part of it, thatched with dead grass, is a firewood stove over which sits a large vessel of sizzling spinach leaves. On the ground, in large aluminium platters are more chopped vegetables. A frail young woman is cooking the evening meal for the whole family. Through eyes filled with smoke she smiles. She is the wife of Mukesh's elder brother. Not much older in years, she has begun to command respect as the bahu, the daughter-in-law of the house, already in charge of three men - her husband, Mukesh and their father, When the older man enters, she gently withdraws behind the broken wall and brings her veil closer to her face. As custom demands, daughters-in-law must veil their faces before male elders. In this case the elder is an impoverished bangle maker. Despite long years of hard labour, first as a tailor, then a bangle maker, he has failed to renovate a house, send his two sons to school. All he has managed to do is teach them what he knows - the art of making bangles.

"It is his karam, his destiny," says Mukesh's grandmother, who has watched her own husband go blind with the dust from polishing the glass of bangles, "Can a god- given lineage ever be broken?" she implies. Born in the caste of bangle makers, they have seen nothing but bangles - in the house, in the yard. In every other house, every other yard, every street in Firozabad. Spirals of bangles - sunny gold, paddy green, royal blue, pink, purple, every colour born out of the seven colours of the rainbow - lie in mounds in unkempt yards, are piled on four-wheeled handcarts, pushed by young men along the narrow lanes of the shanty town. And in dark hutments, next to lines of flames of flickering oil lamps, sit boys and girls with their fathers and mothers, welding pieces of coloured glass into circles of bangles. Their eyes are more adjusted to the dark than to the light outside. This is why they often end up losing their eyesight before they become adults.

Savita, a young girl in a drab pink dress, sits alongside an elderly woman, soldering pieces of glass. As her hands move mechanically like the tongs of a machine, I wonder if she knows the sanctity of the bangles she helps make. It symbolizes an Indian woman's suhaag, auspiciousness in marriage. It will dawn on her suddenly one day when her head is draped with a red veil, her hands dyed red with henna, and red bangles rolled onto her wrists. She will then become a bride, like the old woman beside her who became one many years ago she still has bangles on her wrist, but no light in her eyes, "Ek waqt ser bhar khana bhi nahin khaya," she says, in a voice drained of joy, She has not enjoyed even one full meal in her entire lifetime- that's what she has reaped! Her husband, an old man with a flowing beard, says, "I know nothing except bangles. All I have done is make a house for the family to live in."

Hearing him, one wonders if he has achieved what many have failed in their lifetime. He has a roof over his head!

The cry of not having money to do anything except carry on the business of making bangles, not even enough to eat, rings in every home. The young men echo the lament of their elders. Little has moved with time, it seems, in Firozabad. Years of mind-numbing toil have killed all initiative and the ability to dream.

"Why not organise yourselves into a cooperative?" I ask a group of young men who have fallen into the vicious circle of middlemen who trapped their fathers and forefathers, "Even if we get organized, we are the ones who will be hauled up by the police, beaten and dragged to jail for doing something illegal," they say. There is no leader among them, no one who could help them see things differently. Their fathers are as tired as they are. They talk endlessly in a spiral that moves from poverty to apathy to greed and to injustice.

Listening to them, I see two distinct worlds - one of the family, caught in a web of poverty, burdened by the stigma of caste in which they are born; the other a vicious circle of the sahukars, the middlemen, the policemen, the keepers of law, the bureaucrats and the politicians. Together they have imposed the baggage on the child that he cannot put down. Before he is aware, he accepts it as naturally as his father. To do anything else would mean to dare. And daring is not part of his growing up. When I sense a flash of it in Mukesh I am cheered. "I want to be a motor mechanic,' he repeats. He will go to a garage and learn. But the garage is a long way from his home. "I will walk," he insists. "Do you also dream of flying a plane?" He is suddenly silent. "No", he says, staring at the ground. In his small murmur there is an embarrassment that has not yet turned into regret. He is content to dream of cars that he sees hurtling down the streets of his town. Few airplanes fly over Firozabad.

CHAPTER THREE

Deep Water

It had happened when I was ten or eleven years old. I had decided to learn to swim. There was a pool at the Y.M.C.A. in Yakima that offered exactly the opportunity. The Yakima River was treacherous. Mother continually warned against it, and kept fresh in my mind the details of each drowning in the river. But the Y.M.C.A. pool was safe. It was only two or three feet deep at the shallow end; and while it was nine feet deep at the other, the drop was gradual. I got a pair of water wings and went to the pool. I hated to walknaked into it and show my skinny legs. But I subdued my pride and did it.

From the beginning, however, I had an aversion to the water when I was in it. This started when I was three or four years old and father took me to the beach in California. He and I stood together in the surf. I hung on to him, yet the waves knocked me down and swept over me. I was buried in water. My breath was gone. I was frightened. Father laughed, but there was terror in my heart at the overpowering force of the waves.

My introduction to the Y.M.CA. swimming pool revived unpleasant memories and stirred childish fears. But in a little while I gathered confidence. I paddled with my new water wings, watching the other boys and trying to learn by aping them. I did this two or three times on different days and was just beginning to feel at ease in the water when the misadventure happened.

I went to the pool when no one else was there. The place was quiet. The water was still, and the tiled bottom was as white and clean as a bathtub. I was timid about going in alone, so I sat on the side of the pool to wait for others.

I had not been there long when in came a big bruiser of a boy, probably eighteen years old. He had thick hair on his chest. He was a beautiful physical specimen, with legs and arms that showed rippling muscles. He yelled, "Hi, Skinny! How'd you like to be ducked?

" With that he picked me up and tossed me into the deep end. I landed in a sitting position, swallowed water, and went at once to the bottom. I was frightened, but not yet frightened out of my wits. On the way down I planned: When my feet hit the bottom, I would make a big jump, come to the surface, lie flat on it, and paddle to the edge of the pool.

It seemed a long way down. Those nine feet were more like ninety, and before I touched bottom my lungs were ready to burst. But when my feet hit bottom I summoned all my strength and made what I thought was a great spring upwards. I imagined I would bob to the surface like a cork. Instead, I came up slowly. I opened my eyes and saw nothingbut water — water that had a dirty yellow tinge to it. I grew panicky. I reached up as if to grab a rope and my hands clutched only at water. I was suffocating. I tried to yell but no sound came out. Then my eyes and nose came out of the water — but not my mouth.

I flailed at the surface of the water, swallowed and choked. I tried to bring my legs up, but they hung as dead weights, paralysed and rigid. A great force was pulling me under. I screamed, but only the water heard me. I had started on the long journey back to the bottom of the pool.

I struck at the water as I went down, expending my strength as one in a nightmare fights an irresistible force. I had lost all my breath. My lungs ached, my head throbbed. I was getting dizzy. But I remembered the strategy — I would spring from the bottom of the pool and come like a cork to the surface. I would lie flat on the water, strike out with my arms, and thrash with my legs. Then I would get to the edge of the pool and be safe.

I went down, down, endlessly. I opened my eyes. Nothing but water with a yellow glow — dark water that one could not see through.

And then sheer, stark terror seized me, terror that knows no understanding, terror that knows no control, terror that no one can understand who has not experienced it. I was shrieking under water. I was paralysed under water — stiff, rigid with fear. Even the screams in my throat were frozen. Only my heart, and the pounding in my head, said that I was still alive.

And then in the midst of the terror came a touch of reason. I must remember to jump when I hit the bottom. At last I felt the tiles under me. My toes reached out as if to grab them. I jumped with everything I had.

But the jump made no difference. The water was still around me. I looked for ropes, ladders, water wings. Nothing but water. A mass of yellow water held me. Stark terror took an even deeper hold on me, like a great charge of electricity. I shook and trembled with fright. My arms wouldn't move. My legs wouldn't move. I tried to call for help, to call for mother. Nothing happened.

And then, strangely, there was light. I was coming out of the awful yellow water.

At least my eyes were. My nose was almost out too.

Then I started down a third time. I sucked for air and got water. The yellowish light was going out.

Then all effort ceased. I relaxed. Even my legs felt limp; and a blackness swept over my brain. It wiped out fear; it wiped out terror. There was no more panic. It was quiet and peaceful. Nothing to be afraid of. This is nice... to be drowsy... to go to sleep... no need to jump... too tired to jump... it's nice to be carried gently... to float along in space... tender arms around me... tender arms like Mother's... now I must go to sleep...

I crossed to oblivion, and the curtain of life fell.

The next I remember I was lying on my stomach beside the pool, vomiting. The chap that threw me in was saying, "But I was only fooling." Someone said, "The kid nearly died. Be all right now. Let's carry him to the locker room."

Several hours later, I walked home. I was weak and trembling. I shook and cried when I lay on my bed. I couldn't eat that night. For days a haunting fear was in my heart. The slightest exertion upset me, making me wobbly in the knees and sick to my stomach.

I never went back to the pool. I feared water. I avoided it whenever I could.

A few years later when I came to know the waters of the Cascades, I wanted to get into them. And whenever I did — whether I was wading the Tieton or Bumping River or bathing in Warm Lake of the Goat Rocks — the terror that had seized me in the pool would come back. It would take possession of me completely. My legs would become paralysed. Icy horror would grab my heart.

This handicap stayed with me as the years rolled by. In canoes on Maine lakes fishing for landlocked salmon, bass fishing in New Hampshire, trout fishing on the Deschutes and Metolius in Oregon, fishing for salmon on the Columbia, at Bumping Lake in the Cascades — wherever I went, the haunting fear of the water followed me. It ruined my fishing trips; deprived me of the joy of canoeing, boating, and swimming.

I used every way I knew to overcome this fear, but it held me firmly in its grip. Finally, one October, I decided to get an instructor and learn to swim. I went to a pool and practiced five days a week, an hour each day. The instructor put a belt around me. A rope attached to the belt went through a pulley that ran on an overhead cable. He held on to the end of the rope, and we went back and forth, back and forth across the pool, hour after hour, day after day, week after week. On each trip across the pool a bit of the panic seized me. Each time the instructor relaxed his hold on the rope and I went under, some of the old terror returned and my legs froze. It was three months before the tension began to slack. Then he taught me to put my face under water and exhale, and to raise my nose and inhale. I repeated the exercise hundreds of times. Bit by bit I shed part of the panic that seized me when my head went under water.

Next he held me at the side of the pool and had me kick with my legs. For weeks I did just that. At first my legs refused to work. But they gradually relaxed; and finally I could command them.

Thus, piece by piece, he built a swimmer. And when he had perfected each piece, he put them together into an integrated whole. In April he said, "Now you can swim. Dive off and swim the length of the pool, crawl stroke."

I did. The instructor was finished.

But I was not finished. I still wondered if I would be terror-stricken when I was alone in the pool. I tried it. I swam the length up and down. Tiny vestiges of the old terror would return. But now I could frown and say to that terror, "Trying to scare me, eh? Well, here's to you! Look!" And off I'd go for another length of the pool.

This went on until July. But I was still not satisfied. I was not sure that all the terror had left. So I went to Lake Wentworth in New Hampshire, dived off a dock at Triggs Island, and swam two miles across the lake to Stamp Act Island. I swam the crawl, breast stroke, side stroke, and back stroke. Only once did the terror return. When I was in the middle of the lake, I put my face under and saw nothing but bottomless water. The old sensation returned in miniature. I laughed and said, "Well, Mr Terror, what do you think you can do to me?" It fled and I swam on.

Yet I had residual doubts. At my first opportunity I hurried west, went up the Tieton to Conrad Meadows, up the Conrad Creek Trail to Meade Glacier, and camped in the high meadow by the side of Warm Lake. The next morning I stripped, dived into the lake, and swam across to the other shore and back — just as Doug Corpron used to do. I shouted with joy, and

Gilbert Peak returned the echo. I had conquered my fear of water.

The experience had a deep meaning for me, as only those who have known stark terror and conquered it can appreciate. In death there is peace. There is terror only in the fear of death, as Roosevelt knew when he said, "All we have to fear is fear itself." Because I had experienced both the sensation of dying and the terror that fear of it can produce, the will to live somehow grew in intensity.

At last I felt released — free to walk the trails and climb the peaks and to brush aside fear.

-William o. Douglas

CHAPTER FOUR

The Rattrap

About the writer

Selma Lagerlof was a Swedish writer whose stories have been translated into many languages. A universal theme runs through all of them - a belief that the essential goodness in a human being can be awakened through understanding and love.

Once upon a time there was a man who went around selling small rattraps of wire. He made them himself at odd moments, from the material he got by begging in the stores or at the big farms. But even so, the business was not especially profitable, so he had to resort to both begging and petty thievery to keep body and soul together. Even so, his clothes were in rags, his cheeks were sunken, and hunger gleamed in his eyes. No one can imagine how sad and monotonous life can appear to such a vagabond, who plods along the road, left to his own meditations. But one day this man had fallen into a line of thought, which really seemed to him entertaining. He had naturally been thinking of his rattraps when suddenly he was struck by the idea that the whole world about him - the whole world with its lands and seas, its cities and villages - was nothing but a big rattrap. It had never existed for any other purpose than to set baits for people. It offered riches and joys, shelter and food, heat and clothing, exactly as the rattrap offered cheese and pork, and as soon as anyone let himself be tempted to touch the bait, it closed in on him, and then everything came to an end. The world had, of course, never been very kind to him, so it gave him unwonted joy to think ill of it in this way. It became a cherished pastime of his, during many dreary plodding, to think of people he knew who had let themselves be caught in the dangerous snare, and of others who were still circling around the bait. One dark evening as he was trudging along the road he caught sight of a little gray cottage by the roadside, and he knocked on the door to ask shelter for the night. Nor was he refused. Instead of the sour faces which ordinarily met him, the owner, who was an old man without wife or child, was happy to get someone to talk to in his loneliness. Immediately he put the porridge pot on the fire and gave him supper; then he carved off such a big slice from his tobacco roll that it was enough both for the stranger's pipe and his own. Finally he got out an old pack of cards and played 'mjolis' with his guest until bedtime. The old man was just as generous with his confidences as with his porridge and tobacco. The guest was informed at once that in his days of prosperity his host had been a crofter at Ramsjo Iron works and had worked on the land. Now that he was no longer able to do day labour, it was his cow which supported him. Yes, that bossy was extraordinary. She could give milk for the creamery every day, and last month he had received all of thirty kronor in payment. The stranger must have seemed incredulous, for the old man got up and went to the window, took down a leather pouch which hung on a nail in the very window frame, and picked out three wrinkled ten-krona bills. These he held up before the eyes of his guest, nodding knowingly, and then stuffed them back into the pouch.

The next day both men got up in good season. The crofter was in a hurry to milk his cow, and the other man probably thought he should not stay in bed when the head of the house had gotten up. They left the cottage at the same time. The crofter locked the door and put the key in his pocket. The man with the rattraps said goodbye and thank you, and thereupon each went his own way. But half an hour later the rattrap pedlar stood again before the door. He did not try to get in, however. He only went up to the window, smashed a pane, stuck in his hand, and got hold of the pouch with the thirty kronor. He took the money and thrust it into his own pocket. Then he hung the leather pouch very carefully back in its place and went away. As he walked along with the money in his pocket he felt quite pleased with his smartness. He realized, of course, that at first he dared not continue on the public highway, but must turn off the road, into the woods. During the first hours this caused him no difficulty. Later in the day it became worse, for it was a big and confusing forest which he had gotten into. He tried, to be sure, to walk in a definite direction, but the paths twisted back and forth so strangely! He walked and walked without coming to the end of the wood, and finally he realized that he had only been walking around in the same part of the forest. All at once he recalled his thoughts about the world and the rattrap. Now his own turn had come. He had let himself be fooled by a bait and had been caught. The whole forest, with its trunks and branches, its thickets and fallen logs, closed in upon him like an impenetrable prison from which he could never escape. It was late in December. Darkness was already descending over the forest. This increased the danger, and increased also his gloom and despair. Finally he saw no way out, and he sank down on the ground, tired to death, thinking that his last moment had come. But just as he laid his head on the ground, he heard a sound - a hard regular thumping. There was no doubt as to what that was. He raised himself. ""Those are the hammer strokes from an iron mill", he thought. ""There must be people nearby". He summoned all his strength, got up, and staggered in the direction of the sound. The Ramsjo Ironworks, which are now closed down, were, not so long ago, a large plant, with smelter, rolling mill, and forge. In the summertime long lines of heavily loaded barges and scows slid down the canal, which led to a large inland lake, and in the wintertime the roads near the mill were black from all the coal dust which sifted down from the big charcoal crates. During one of the long dark evenings just before Christmas, the master smith and his helper sat in the dark forge near the furnace waiting for the pig iron, which had been put in the fire, to be ready to put on the anvil. Every now and then one of them got up to stir the glowing mass with a long iron bar, returning in a few moments, dripping with perspiration, though, as was the custom, he wore nothing but a long shirt and a pair of wooden shoes. All the time there were many sounds to be heard in the forge. The big bellows groaned and the burning coal cracked. The fire boy shovelled charcoal into the maw of the furnace with a great deal of clatter. Outside roared the waterfall, and a sharp north wind whipped the rain against the brick- tiled roof. It was probably on account of all this noise that the blacksmith did not notice that a man had opened the gate and entered the forge, until he stood close up to the furnace. Surely it was nothing unusual for poor vagabonds without any better shelter for the night to be attracted to the forge by the glow of light which escaped through the sooty panes, and to come in to warm themselves in front of the fire. The blacksmiths glanced only casually and indifferently at the intruder. He looked the way people of his type usually did, with a long beard, dirty, ragged, and with a bunch of rattraps dangling on his chest. He asked permission to stay, and the master blacksmith nodded a haughty consent without honouring him with a single word. The tramp did not say anything, either. He had not come there to talk but only to warm himself and sleep.

In those days the Ramsjo iron mill was owned by a very prominent ironmaster, whose greatest ambition was to ship out good iron to the market. He watched both night and day to see that the work was done as well as possible, and at this very moment he came into the forge on one of his nightly rounds of inspection. Naturally the first thing he saw was the tall raga muffin who had eased his way so close to the furnace that steam rose from his wet rags. The ironmaster did not follow the example of the blacksmiths, who had hardly deigned to look at the stranger. He walked close up to him, looked him over very carefully, and then tore off his slouch hat to get a better view of his face. "But of course it is you, Nils O loft!" he said. "How you do look!" The man with the rattraps had never before seen their own master at Ramsjo and did not even know what his name was. But it occurred to him that if the fine gentleman thought he was an old acquaintance, he might perhaps throw him a couple of kronor. Therefore he did not want to undeceive him all at once. ""Yes, God knows things have gone downhill with me"', he said. "You should not have resigned from the regiment', said the ironmaster. "That was the mistake. If only I had still been in the service at the time, it never would have happened. Well, now of course you will come home with me." To go along up to the manor house and be received by the owner like an old regimental comrade - that, however, did not please the tramp. 'No, I couldn't think of it!" he said, looking quite alarmed. He thought of the thirty kronor. To go up to the manor house would be like throwing himself voluntarily into the lion's den. He only wanted a chance to sleep here in the forge and then sneak away as inconspicuously as possible. The ironmaster assumed that he felt embarrassed because of his miserable clothing. "Please don't think that I have such a fine home that you cannot show yourself there', He said... "Elizabeth is dead, as you may already have heard. My boys are abroad, and there is no one at home except my oldest daughter and myself. We were just saying that it was too bad we didn't have any company for Christmas. Now come along with me and help us make the Christmas food disappear a little faster." But the stranger said no, and no, and again no, and the iron master saw that he must give in. "It looks as though Captain von Stanley preferred to stay with you tonight, Stjernstrom"', he said to the master blacksmith, and turned on his heel. But he laughed to himself as he went away, and the blacksmith, who knew him, understood very well that he had not said his last word. It was not more than half an hour before they heard the sound of carriage wheels outside the forge, and a new guest came in, but this time it was not the ironmaster. He had sent his daughter, apparently hoping that she would have better power of persuasion than he himself. She entered, followed by a valet, carrying on his arm a big fur coat. She was not at all pretty, but seemed modest and quite shy. In the forge everything was just as it had been earlier in the evening. The master blacksmith and his apprentice still sat on their bench, and iron and charcoal still glowed in the furnace. The stranger had stretched himself out on the floor and lay with a piece of pig iron under his head and his hat pulled down over his eyes. As soon as the young girl caught sight of him, she went up and lifted his hat. The man was evidently used to sleeping with one eye open. He jumped up abruptly and seemed to be quite frightened. "My name is Edla Willmansson," said the young girl. ""My father came home and said that you wanted to sleep here in the forge tonight, and then I asked permission to come and bring you home to us. I am so sorry, Captain, that you are having such a hard time." She looked at him compassionately, with her heavy eyes, and then she noticed that the man was afraid. "Either he has stolen something or else he has escaped from jail"', she thought, and added quickly, ""You may be sure, Captain, that you will be allowed to leave us just as freely as you came. Only please stay with us over Christmas Eve." She said this in such a friendly manner that the rattrap pedlar must have felt confidence in her. "It would never have occurred to me that you would bother with me yourself, miss,"' he said. "I will come at once." He accepted the fur coat, which the valet handed him with a deep bow, threw it over his rags, and followed the young lady out to the carriage, without granting the astonished blacksmiths so much as a glance. But while he was riding up to the manorhouse he had evil forebodings. "Why the devil did I take that fellow's money?" he thought. "Now I am sitting in the trap and will never get out of it." The next day was Christmas Eve, and when their own master came into the dining room for breakfast he probably thought with satisfaction of his old regimental comrade whom he had run across so unexpectedly."First of all we must see to it that he gets a little flesh on his bones," he said to his daughter, who was busy at the table. "And then we must see that he gets something else to do than to run around the country selling rattraps."' "It is queer that things have gone downhill with him as badly as that," said the daughter. "Last night I did not think there was anything about him to show that he had once been an educated man." "You must have patience, my little girl," said the father. "As soon as he gets clean and dressed up, you will see something different. Last night he was naturally embarrassed. The tramp manners will fall away from him with the tramp clothes." Just as he said this the door opened and the stranger entered. Yes, now he was truly clean and well dressed. The valet had bathed him, cut his hair, and shaved him. Moreover he was dressed in a good-looking suit of clothes which belonged to the ironmaster. He wore a white shirt and a starched collar and whole shoes. But although his guest was now so well groomed, their own master did not seem pleased. He looked at him with puckered brow, and it was easy to understand that when he had seen the strange fellow in the uncertain reflection from the furnace he might have made a mistake, but that now, when he stood there in broad daylight, it was impossible to mistake him for an old acquaintance. ""What does this mean?" he thundered. The stranger made no attempt to dissimulate. He saw at once that the splendor had come to an end.

"It is not my fault, sir," he said. "I never pretended to be anything but a poor trader, and I pleaded and begged to be allowed to stay in the forge. But no harm has been done. At worst I can put on my rags again and go away"'. "Well," said the ironmaster, hesitating a little, "it was not quite honest, either. You must admit that, and I should not be surprsed if the sheriff would like to have something to say in the matter." The tramp took a step forward and struck the table with his fist. "Now I am going to tell you, Mr. Ironmaster, how things are," he said. ""This whole world is nothing but a big rattrap. All the good things that are offered to you are nothing but cheese rinds and bits of pork, set out to drag a poor fellow into trouble. And if the sheriff comes now and locks me up for this, then you, Mr. Ironmaster, must remember that a day may come when you yourself may want to get a big piece of pork, and then you will get caught in the trap." The ironmaster began to laugh. 'That was not so badly said, my good fellow. Perhaps we should let the sheriff alone on Christmas Eve. But now get out of here as fast as you can." But just as the man was opening the door, the daughter said, "I think he ought to stay with us today. I don't want him to go." And with that she went and closed the door. "What in the world are you doing?" said the father. The daughter stood there quite embarrassed and hardly knew what to answer. That morning she had felt so happy when she thought how homelike and Christmassy she was going to make things for the poor hungry wretch. She could not get away from the idea all at once, and that was why she had interceded for the vagabond. "I am thinking of this stranger here," said the young girl. "He walks and walks the whole year long and there is probably not a single place in the whole country where he is welcome and can feel at home. Wherever he turns he is chased away. Always he is afraid of being arrested and cross examined. I should like to have him enjoy a day of peace with us here - Just one in the whole year." The ironmaster mumbled something in his beard. He could not bring himself to oppose her. "It was all a mistake, of course," she continued. "But anyway I don't think we ought to chase away a human being whom we have asked to come here, and to whom we have promised Christmas cheer." "You do preach worse than a parson," said their own master. "I only hope you won't have to regret this.

" The young girl took the stranger by the hand and led him up to the table. ""Now sit down and eat,' she said, for she could see that her father had given in. The man with the rattraps said not a word; he only sat down and helped himself to the food. Time after time, he looked at the young girl who had interceded for him. Why had she done it? What could the crazy idea be? After that, Christmas Eve at Ramsjo passed just as it always had. The stranger did not cause any trouble because he did nothing but sleep. The whole forenoon he lay on the sofa in one of the guest rooms and slept at one stretch. At noon they woke him up so that he could have his share of the good Christmas fare, but after that he slept again. It seemed as though for many years he had not been able to sleep as quietly and safely as here at Ramsjo. In the evening, when the Christmas tree was lighted, they woke him up again, and he stood for a while in the drawing room, blinking as though the candlelight hurt him, but after that he disappeared again. Two hours later he was aroused once more. He then had to go down into the dining room and eat the Christmas fish and porridge. As soon as they got up from the table he went around to each one present and said thank you and good night, but when he came to the young girl she gave him to understand that it was her father's intention that the suit which he wore was to be a Christmas present - he did not have to return it; and if he wanted to spend next Christmas Eve in a place where he could rest in peace, and be sure that no evil would befall him, he would be welcomed back again. The man with the rattraps did not answer anything to this. He only stared at the young girl in boundless amazement. The next morning their own master and his daughter got up in good season to go to the early Christmas service. Their guest was still asleep, and they did not disturb him. When, at about ten o'clock, they drove back from the church, the young girl sat and hung her head even more dejectedly than usual. At church she had learned that one of the old crofters of the ironworks had been robbed by a man who went around selling rattraps. "Yes, that was a fine fellow you let into the house," said her father. "I only wonder how many silver spoons are left in the cupboard by this time." The wagon had hardly stopped at the front steps when the ironmaster asked the valet whether the stranger was still there. He added that he had heard at church that the man was a thief. The valet answered that the fellow had gone and that he had not taken anything with him at all. On the contrary, he had left behind a little package which Miss Willmansson was to be kind enough to accept as a Christmas present. The young girl opened the package, which was so badly done up that the contents came into view at once. She gave a little cry of joy. She found a small rattrap, and in it lay three wrinkled ten kronor notes. But that was not all. In the rattrap lay also a letter written in large, jagged characters - 'Honored and noble Miss, Since you have been so nice to me all day long, as if I was a captain, I want to be nice to you, in return, as if I was areal captain - for I do not want you to be embarrassed at this Christmas season by a thief; but you can give back the money to the old man on the roadside, who has the money pouch hanging on the window frame as a bait for poor wanderers. "The rattrap is a Christmas present from a rat who would have been caught in this world's rattrap if he had not been raised to captain, because in that way he got power to clear himself". Written with friendship and high regard, "Captain von Stahle"'.

CHAPTER FIVE

Indigo

When I first visited Gandhi in 1942 at his ashram in Sevagram, in central India, he said, "I will tell you how it happened that I decided to urge the departure of the British. It was in 1917."

He had gone to the December 1916 annual convention of the Indian National Congress party in Lucknow. There were 2301 delegates and many visitors. During the proceedings, Gandhi recounted, "A peasant came up to me looking like any other peasant in India, poor and emaciated, and said, 'I am Rajkumar Shukla. I am from Champaran, and I want you to come to my district"! Gandhi had never heard of the place. It was in the foothills of the towering Himalayas, near the kingdom of Nepal.

Under an ancient arrangement, the Champaran peasants were sharecroppers. Rajkumar Shukla was one of them. He was illiterate but resolute. He had come to the Congress session to complain about the injustice of the landlord system in Bihar and somebody had probably said, "Speak to Gandhi".

Gandhi told Shukla he had an appointment in Cawnpore and was also committed to go to other parts of India. Shukla accompanied him everywhere. Then Gandhi returned to his ashram near Ahmedabad. Shukla followed him to the ashram. For weeks he never left Gandhi's side.

"Fixe date," he begged.

Impressed by the sharecropper's tenacity and story Gandhi said, "I have to be in Calcutta on such-and-such a date. Come and meet me and take me from there."

Months passed. Shukla was sitting on his haunches at the appointed spot in Calcutta when Gandhi arrived; he waited till Gandhi was free. Then the two of them boarded a train for the city of Patna in Bihar. There Shukla led him to the house of a lawyer named Rajendra Prasad who later became President of the Congress party and of India. Rajendra Prasad was out of town, but the servants knew Shukla as a poor yeoman who pestered their master to help the indigo sharecroppers. So they let him stay on the grounds with his companion, Gandhi, whom they took to be another peasant. But Gandhi was not permitted to draw water from the well lest some drops from his bucket pollute the entire source; how did they know that he was not an untouchable?

Gandhi decided to go first to Muzzafarpur, which was en route to Champaran, to obtain more (complete) information about the conditions than Shukla was capable of imparting. He accordingly sent a telegram to Professor J.B. Kripalani, of the Arts College in Muzzafarpur, whom he had seen at Tagore's Shantiniketan school. The train arrived at midnight, 15 April 1917. Kripalani was waiting at the station with a large body of students. Gandhi stayed there for two days in the home of Professor Malkani, a teacher in a government school. "It was an extraordinary thing in those days," Gandhi commented, "for a government professor to harbour a man like me". In smaller localities, the Indians were afraid to show sympathy for advocates of home-rule.

The news of Gandhi's advent and of the nature of his mission spread quickly through Muzzatarpur and to Champaran. Sharecroppers from Champaran began arriving on foot and by conveyance to see their champion. Muzzafarpur lawyers called on Gandhi to brief him; they frequently represented peasant groups in court; they told him about their cases and reported the size of their fee.

Gandhi chided the lawyers for collecting big fee from the sharecroppers. He said, "I have come to the conclusion that we should stop going to law courts. Taking such cases to the courts does little good. Where the peasants are so crushed and fear- stricken, law courts are useless. The real relief for them is to be free from fear."

Most of the arable land in the Champaran district was divided into large estates owned by Englishmen and worked by Indian tenants. The chief commercial crop was indigo. The landlords compelled all tenants to plant three twentieths or 15 percent of their holdings with indigo and surrender the entire indigo harvest as rent. This was done by a long-term contract.

Presently, the landlords learned that Germany had developed synthetic indigo. They thereupon, obtained agreements from the sharecroppers to pay them compensation for being released from the 15 per cent arrangement.

The sharecropping arrangement was irksome to the peasants, and many signed willingly. Those who resisted, engaged lawyers; the landlords hired thugs. Meanwhile, the information about synthetic indigo reached the illiterate peasants who had signed, and they wanted their money back.

At this point Gandhi arrived in Champaran.

He began by trying to get the facts. First he visited the secretary of the British landlord's association. The Secretary told him that they could give no information to an outsider. Gandhi answered that he was no outsider.

Next, Gandhi called on the British official commissioner of the Tirhut division in which the Champaran district lay. "The commissioner," Gandhi reports, "proceeded to bully me and advised me forthwith to leave Tirhut".

Gandhi did not leave. Instead he proceeded to Motihari, the capital of Champaran. Several lawyers accompanied him. At the railway station, a vast multitude greeted Gandhi. He went to a house and using it as headquarters, continued his investigations. A report came in that a peasant had been maltreated in a nearby village. Gandhi decided to go and see; the next morning he started out on the back of an elephant. He had not proceeded far when the police superintendent's messenger overtook him and ordered him to return to town in his carriage. Gandhi complied. The messenger drove Gandhi home where he served him with an official notice to quit Champaran immediately. Gandhi signed a receipt for the notice and wrote on it

that he would disobey the order.

In consequence, Gandhi received summon to appear in court the next day.

All night Gandhi remained awake. He telegraphed Rajendra Prasad to come from Bihar with influential friends. He sent instructions to the ashram. He wired a full report to the Viceroy.

Morning found the town of Motihari black with peasants. They did not know Gandhi's record in South Africa. They had merely heard that a Mahatma who wanted to help them was in trouble with the authorities. Their spontaneous demonstration, in thousands, around the courthouse was the beginning of their liberation from fear of the British.

The officials felt powerless without Gandhi's cooperation. He helped them regulate the crowd. He was polite and friendly. He was giving them concrete proof that their might, hitherto dreaded and unquestioned, could be challenged by Indians.

The government was baffled. The prosecutor requested the judge to postpone the trial. Apparently, the authorities wished to consult their superiors.

Gandhi protested against the delay. He read a statement pleading guilty. He was involved, he told the court, in a "conflict of duties" - on the one hand, not to set a bad example as a lawbreaker; on the other hand, to render the "humanitarian and national

service" for which he had come. He disregarded the order to leave, "not for want of respect for lawful authority, but in obedience to the higher law of our being, the voice of conscience". He asked the penalty due.

The magistrate announced that he would pronounce sentence after a two-hour recess and asked Gandhi to furnish bail for those i20 minutes. Gandhi refused. The judge released him without bail.

When the court reconvened, the judge said he would not deliver the judgement for several days. Meanwhile he allowed Gandhi to remain at liberty.

Rajendra Prasad, Brij Kishor Babu, Maulana Mazharul Hug and several other prominent lawyers had arrived from Bihar. They conferred with Gandhi. What would they doif he was sentenced to prison, Gandhi asked. Why, the senior lawyer replied, they had come to advise and help him; if he went to jail there would be nobody to advise and they would go home.

What about the injustice to the sharecroppers, Gandhi demanded? The lawyers withdrew to consult. Rajendra Prasad has recorded the upshot of their consultations - "They thought, amongst themselves, that Gandhi was totally a stranger, and yet he was prepared to go to prison for the sake of the peasants; if they, on the other hand, being not only residents of the adjoining districts but also those who claimed to have served these peasants, should go home, it would be shameful desertion."

They accordingly went back to Gandhi and told him they were ready to follow him into jail. "The battle of Champaran is won," he exclaimed. Then he took a piece of paper and divided the group into pairs and put down the order in which each pair was to court arrest.

Several days later, Gandhi received a written communication from the magistrate informing him that the Lieutenant-Governor of the province had ordered the case to be dropped. Civil Disobedience had triumphed, the first time in modern India.

Gandhi and the lawyers now proceeded to conduct a far-flung inquiry into the erievances of the farmers. Depositions by about ten thousand peasants were written down, and notes made on other evidence. Documents were collected. The whole area throbbed with the activity of the investigators and the vehement protests of the landlords.

In June, Gandhi was summoned by Sir Edward Gait, the Lieutenant - Governor. Before he went he met leading associates and again laid detailed plans for Civil Disobedience if he should not return.

Gandhi had four protracted interviews with the Lieutenant - Governor who, as a result, appointed an official commission of inquiry into the indigo sharecroppers' situation. The commission consisted of landlords, government officials, and Gandhi as the sole representative of the peasants. Gandhi remained in Champaran for an initial uninterrupted period of seven months and then again for several shorter visits. The visit, undertaken casually on the entreaty of an unlettered peasant in the expectation that it would last a few days, occupied almost a year of Gandhi's life.

The official inquiry assembled a crushing mountain of evidence against the big planters, and when they saw this they agreed, in principle, to make refunds to the peasants. "But how much must we pay?" they asked Gandhi.

They thought he would demand repayment in full of the money which they had illegally and deceitfully extorted from the sharecroppers. He asked only 50 per cent. "There he seemed adamant," writes Reverend J.Z. Hodge, a British missionary in Champaran who observed the entire episode at close range. "Thinking probably that he would not give way, the representative of the planters offered to refund to the extent of 25 percent, and to his amazement Mr. Gandhi took him at his word, thus breaking the deadlock."

This settlement was adopted unanimously by the commission. Gandhi explained that the amount of the refund was less important than the fact that the landlords had been obliged to surrender part of the money and, with it, part of their prestige. Therefore, as far as the peasants were concerned, the planters had behaved as lords above the law. Now the peasant saw that he had rights and defenders. He learned courage.

Events justified Gandhi's position. Within a few years the British planters abandoned their estates, which reverted to the peasants. Indigo sharecropping disappeared.

Gandhi never contented himself with large political or economic solutions. He saw the cultural and social backwardness in the Champaran villages and wanted to do something about it immediately. He appealed to teachers. Mahadev Desai and Narhari Parikh, two young men who had just joined Gandhi as disciples, and their wives, volunteered for the work.

Several more came from Bombay, Poona and other distant parts of the land. Devadas, Gandhi's youngest son, arrived from the ashram and so did Mrs. Gandhi. Primary schools were opened in six villages. Kasturba taught the ashram rules on personal cleanliness and community sanitation.

Health conditions were miserable. Gandhi got a doctor to volunteer his services for six months. Three medicines were available - castor oil, quinine and sulphur - ointment. Anybody who showed a coated tongue was given a dose of castor oil; anybody with malaria fever received quinine plus castor oil; anybody with skin eruptions received ointment plus castor oil.

Gandhi noticed the filthy state of women's clothes. He asked Kasturba to talk to them about it. One woman took Kasturba into her hut and said, "Look, there is no box or cupboard here for clothes. The sari I am wearing is the only one I have."

During his long stay in Champaran, Gandhi kept a long distance watch on the ashram. He sent regular instructions by mail and asked for financial accounts. Once he wrote to the residents that it was time to fill in the old latrine trenches and dig new ones otherwise the old ones would begin to smell bad.

The Champaran episode was a turning-point in Gandhi's life. "What I did," he explained, "was a very ordinary thing. I declared that the British could not order me about in my own country."

But Champaran did not begin as an act of defiance. It grew out of an attempt to alleviate the distress of large number of poor peasants. This was the typical Gandhi pattern - his politics were intertwined with the practical, day-to-day problems of the millions. His was not a loyalty to abstractions; it was a loyalty to living, human beings.

In everything Gandhi did, moreover, he tried to mould a new free Indian who could stand on his own feet and thus make India free.

Early in the Champaran action, Charles Freer Andrews, the English pacifist who had become a devoted follower of the Mahatma, came to bid Gandhi farewell before going on a tour of duty to the Fiji Islands. Gandhi's lawyer friends thought it would be a good idea for Andrews to stay in Champaran and help them. Andrews was willing if Gandhi agreed. But Gandhi was vehemently opposed. He said, "You think that in this unequal fight it would be helpful if we have an Englishman on our side. This shows the weakness of your heart. The cause is just and you must rely upon yourself to win the battle. You should not seek a prop in Mr. Andrews because he happens to be an Englishman."

"He had read our minds correctly," Rajendra Prasad commented, "and we had no reply...... Gandhi in this way taught us a lesson in self-reliance." Self-reliance, Indian independence and help to sharecroppers were all bound together.

CHAPTER SIX

The Third Level

The presidents of the New York Central and the New York, New Haven and Hartford railroads will swear on a stack of timetables that there are only two. But I say there are three, because I've been on the third level of the Grand Central Station. Yes, I've taken the obvious step: I talked to a psychiatrist friend of mine, among others. I told him about the third level at Grand Central Station, and he said it was a wakingdream wish fulfillment. He said I was unhappy. That made my wife kind of mad, but he explained that he meant the modern world is full of insecurity, fear, war, worry and all the rest of it, and that I just want to escape. Well, who doesn't? Everybody I know wants to escape, but they don't wander down into any third level at Grand Central Station.

But that's the reason, he said, and my friends all agreed. Everything points to it, they claimed. My stamp collecting, for example; that's a 'temporary refuge from reality.' Well, maybe, but my grandfather didn't need any refuge from reality; things were pretty nice and peaceful in his day, from all I hear, and he started my collection. It's a nice collection too, blocks of four of practically every U.S. issue, first-day covers, and so on. President Roosevelt collected stamps too, you know.

Anyway, here's what happened at Grand Central. One night last summer I worked late at the office. I was in a hurry to get uptown to my apartment so I decided to take the subway from Grand Central because it's faster than the bus.

Now, I don't know why this should have happened to me. I'm just an ordinary guy named Charley, thirty-one years old, and I was wearing a tan gabardine suit and a straw hat with a fancy band; I passed a dozen men who looked just like me. And I wasn't trying to escape from anything; I just wanted to get home to Louisa, my wife.

I turned into Grand Central from Vanderbilt Avenue, and went down the steps to the first level, where you take trains like the Twentieth Century. Then I walked down another flight to the second level, where the suburban trains leave from, ducked into an arched doorway heading for the subway — and got lost. That's easy to do. I've been in and out of Grand Central hundreds of times, but I'm always bumping into new doorways and stairs and corridors. Once I got into a tunnel about a mile long and came out in the lobby of the Roosevelt Hotel. Another time I came up in an office building on Forty-sixth Street, three blocks away.

Sometimes I think Grand Central is growing like a tree, pushing out new corridors and staircases like roots. There's probably a long tunnel that nobody knows about feeling its way under the city right now, on its way to Times Square, and maybe another to Central Park. And maybe — because for so many people through the years Grand Central has been an exit, a way of escape — maybe that's how the tunnel I got into... But I never told my psychiatrist friend about that idea. The corridor I was in began angling left and slanting downward and I thought that was wrong, but I kept on walking. All I could hear was the empty sound of my own footsteps and I didn't pass a soul. Then I heard that sort of hollow roar ahead that means open space and people talking. The tunnel turned sharp left; I went down a short flight of stairs and came out on the third level at Grand Central Station. For just a moment I thought I was back on the second level, but I saw the room was smaller, there were fewer ticket windows and train gates, and the information booth in the centre was wood and oldlooking. And the man in the booth wore a green eyeshade and long black sleeve protectors. The lights were dim and sort of flickering. Then I saw why; they were open-flame gaslights. There were brass spittoons on the floor, and across the station a glint of light caught my eye; a man was pulling a gold watch from his vest pocket. He snapped open the cover, glanced at his watch and frowned. He wore a derby hat, a black four-button suit with tiny lapels, and he had a big, black, handlebar mustache. Then I looked around and saw that everyone in the station was dressed like eighteen-ninety-something; I never saw so many beards, sideburns and fancy mustaches in my life. A woman walked in through the train gate; she wore a dress with leg-ofmutton sleeves and skirts to the top of her high-buttoned shoes. Back of her, out on the tracks, I caught a glimpse of a locomotive, a very small Currier & Ives locomotive with a funnel-shaped stack. And then I knew. To make sure, I walked over to a newsboy and glanced at the stack of papers at his feet. It was The World; and The World hasn't been published for years. The lead story said something about President Cleveland. I've found that front page since, in the Public Library files, and it was printed June 11, 1894. I turned toward the ticket windows knowing that here — on the third level at Grand Central — I could buy tickets that would take Louisa and me anywhere in the United States we wanted to go. In the year 1894. And I wanted two tickets to Galesburg, Illinois. Have you ever been there? It's a wonderful town still, with big old frame houses, huge lawns, and tremendous trees whose branches meet overhead and roof the streets. And in 1894, summer evenings were twice as long, and people sat out on their lawns, the men smoking cigars and talking quietly, the women waving palm-leaf fans, with the fire-flies all around, in a peaceful world. To be back here with the First World War still twenty years off, and World War II over forty years in the future... I wanted two tickets for that. The clerk figured the fare — he glanced at my fancy hatband, but he figured the fare — and I had enough for two coach tickets, one way. But when I counted out the money and looked up, the clerk was staring at me. He nodded at the bills. "That ain't money, mister," he said, "and if you're trying to skin me, you won't get very far," and he glanced at the cash drawer beside him. Of course the money was old-style bills, half again as big as the money we use nowadays, and different-looking. I turned away and got out fast. There's nothing nice about jail, even in 1894. And that was that. I left the same way I came, I suppose. Next day, during lunch hour, I drew three hundred dollars out of the bank, nearly all we had, and bought old-style currency (that really worried my psychiatrist friend). You can buy old money at almost any coin dealer's, but you have to pay a premium. My three hundred dollars bought less than two hundred in old-style bills, but I didn't care; eggs were thirteen cents a dozen in 1894. But I've never again found the corridor that leads to the third level at Grand Central Station, although I've tried often enough. Louisa was pretty worried when I told her all this, and didn't want me to look for the third level any more, and after a while I stopped; I went back to my stamps. But now we're both looking, every weekend, because now we have proof that the third level is still there. My friend Sam Weiner disappeared! Nobody knew where, but I sort of suspected because Sam's a city boy, and I used to tell him about Galesburg — I went to school there — and he always said he liked the sound of the place. And that's where he is, all right. In 1894. Because one night, fussing with my stamp collection, I found — Well, do you know what a first-day cover is? When a new stamp is issued, stamp collectors buy some and use them to mail envelopes to themselves on the very first day of sale; and the postmark proves the date. The envelope is called a first-day cover. They're never opened; you just put blank paper in the envelope. That night, among my oldest first-day covers, I found one that shouldn't have been there. But there it was. It was there because someone had mailed it to my grandfather at his home in Galesburg; that's what the address on the envelope said. And it had been there since July 18, 1894 — the postmark showed that — yet I didn't remember it at all. The stamp was a six-cent, dull brown, with a picture of President Garfield. Naturally, when the envelope came to Granddad in the mail, it went right into his collection and stayed there — till I took it out and opened it. The paper inside wasn't blank. It read: The note is signed Sam. At the stamp and coin store I go to, I found out that Sam bought eight hundred dollars' worth of old-style currency. That ought to set him up in a nice little hay, feed and grain business; he always said that's what he really wished he could do, and he certainly can't go back to his old business. Not in Galesburg, Illinois, in 1894. His old business? Why, Sam was my psychiatrist.

CHAPTER SEVEN

The Tiger King

The Maharaja of Pratibandapuram is the hero of this story. He may be identified as His Highness Jamedar-General, Khiledar-Major, Sata Vyaghra Samhari, Maharajadhiraja Visva Bhuvana Samrat, Sir Jilani Jung Jung Bahadur, M.A.D., A.C.T.C., or C.R.C.K. But this name is often shortened to the Tiger King. I have come forward to tell you why he came to be known as Tiger King. I have no intention of pretending to advance only to end in a strategic withdrawal. Even the threat of a Stuka bomber will not throw me off track. The Stuka, if it likes, can beat a hasty retreat from my story. Right at the start, it is imperative to disclose a matter of vital importance about the Tiger King. Everyone who reads of him will experience the natural desire to meet a man of his indomitable courage face-to-face. But there is no chance of its fulfilment.

As Bharata said to Rama about Dasaratha, the Tiger King has reached that final abode of all living creatures. In other words, the Tiger King is dead. The manner of his death is a matter of extraordinary interest. It can be revealed only at the end of the tale. The most fantastic aspect of his demise was that as soon as he was born, astrologers had foretold that one day the Tiger King would actually have to die. "The child will grow up to become the warrior of warriors, hero of heroes, champion of champions. But..." they bit their lips and swallowed hard. When compelled to continue, the astrologers came out with it.

"This is a secret which should not be revealed at all. And yet we are forced to speak out. The child born under this star will one day have to meet its death." At that very moment a great miracle took place. An astonishing phrase emerged from the lips of the ten-dayold Jilani Jung Jung Bahadur, "O wise prophets!" Everyone stood transfixed in stupefaction. They looked wildly at each other and blinked. "O wise prophets! It was I who spoke." This time there were no grounds for doubt. It was the infant born just ten days ago who had enunciated the words so clearly. The chief astrologer took off his spectacles and gazed intently at the baby. "All those who are born will one day have to die. We don't need your predictions to know that. There would be some sense in it if you could tell us the manner of that death," the royal infant uttered these words in his little squeaky voice. The chief astrologer placed his finger on his nose in wonder. A baby barely ten days old opens its lips in speech! Not only that, it also raises intelligent questions! Incredible! Rather like the bulletins issued by the war office, than facts.

The chief astrologer took his finger off his nose and fixed his eyes upon the little prince. "The prince was born in the hour of the Bull. The Bull and the Tiger are enemies, therefore, death comes from the Tiger," he explained. You may think that crown prince Jung Jung Bahadur was thrown into a quake when he heard the word 'Tiger'. That was exactly what did not happen. As soon as he heard it pronounced, the crown prince gave a deep growl. Terrifying words emerged from his lips. "Let tigers beware!" This account is only a rumour rife in Pratibandapuram. But with hindsight we may conclude it was based on some truth. Crown prince Jung Jung Bahadur grew taller and stronger day by day.

No other miracle marked his childhood days apart from the event already described. The boy drank the milk of an English cow, was brought up by an English nanny, tutored in English by an Englishman, saw nothing but English films — exactly as the crown princes of all the other Indian states did. When he came of age at twenty, the State, which had been with the Court of Wards until then, came into his hands. But everyone in the kingdom remembered the astrologer's prediction. Many continued to discuss the matter. Slowly it came to the Maharaja's ears. There were innumerable forests in the Pratibandapuram State. They had tigers in them. The Maharaja knew the old saying, 'You may kill even a cow in self-defence'. There could certainly be no objection to killing tigers in self-defence. The Maharaja started out on a tiger hunt.

The Maharaja was thrilled beyond measure when he killed his first tiger. He sent for the State astrologer and showed him the dead beast. "What do you say now?" he demanded. "Your majesty may kill ninety-nine tigers in exactly the same manner. But..." the astrologer drawled.

"But what? Speak without fear." "But you must be very careful with the hundredth tiger. "What if the hundredth tiger were also killed?" "Then I will tear up all my books on astrology, set fire to them, and..." "And..." "I shall cut off my tuft, crop my hair short and become an insurance agent," the astrologer finished on an incoherent note.

III

From that day onwards it was celebration time for all the tigers inhabiting Pratibandapuram. The State banned tiger hunting by anyone except the Maharaja. A proclamation was issued to the effect that if anyone dared to fling so much as a stone at a tiger, all his wealth and property would be confiscated. The Maharaja vowed he would attend to all other matters only after killing the hundred tigers. Initially the king seemed well set to realise his ambition. Not that he faced no dangers. There were times when the bullet missed its mark, the tiger leapt upon him and he fought the beast with his bare hands. Each time it was the Maharaja who won. At another time he was in danger of losing his throne. A high-ranking British officer visited Pratibandapuram. He was very fond of hunting tigers. And fonder of being photographed with the tigers he had shot. As usual, he wished to hunt tigers in Pratibandapuram.

But the Maharaja was firm in his resolve. He refused permission. "I can organise any other hunt. You may go on a boar hunt. You may conduct a mouse hunt. We are ready for a mosquito hunt. But tiger hunt! That's impossible!" The British officer's secretary sent word to the Maharaja through the dewan that the durai himself did not have to kill the tiger. The Maharaja could do the actual killing. What was important to the durai was a photograph of himself holding the gun and standing over the tiger's carcass. But the Maharaja would not agree even to this proposal. If he relented now, what would he do if other British officers turned up for tiger hunts?

Because he prevented a British officer from fulfilling his desire, the Maharaja stood in danger of losing his kingdom itself. The Maharaja and the dewan held deliberations over this issue. As a result, a telegram was despatched forthwith to a famous British company of jewellers in Calcutta.

'Send samples of expensive diamond rings of different designs.' Some fifty rings arrived. The Maharaja sent the whole lot to the British officer's good lady. The king and the minister expected the duraisani to choose one or two rings and send the rest back. Within no time at all the duraisani sent her reply: 'Thank you very much for your gifts.' In two days a bill for three lakh of rupees came from the British jewellers. The Maharaja was happy that though he had lost three lakh of rupees, he had managed to retain his kingdom.

IV

The Maharaja's tiger hunts continued to be highly successful. Within ten years he was able to kill seventy tigers. And then, an unforeseen hurdle brought his mission to a standstill. The tiger population became extinct in the forests of Pratibandapuram. Who knows whether the tigers practised birth control or committed harakiri? Or simply ran away from the State because they desired to be shot by British hands alone? One day the Maharaja sent for the dewan. "Dewan saheb, aren't you aware of the fact that thirty tigers still remain to be shot down by this gun of mine?" he asked brandishing his gun. Shuddering at the sight of the gun, the dewan cried out, "Your Majesty! I am not a tiger!" "Which idiot would call you a tiger?" "No, and I'm not a gun!" "You are neither tiger nor gun. Dewan saheb, I summoned you here for a different purpose. I have decided to get married." The dewan began to babble even more. "Your Majesty, I have two wives already. If I marry you ..." "Don't talk nonsense! Why should I marry you? What I want is a tiger..." "Your Majesty! Please think it over. Your ancestors were married to the sword. If you like, marry the gun. A Tiger King is more than enough for this state. It doesn't need a Tiger Queen as well!" The Maharaja gave a loud crack of laughter. "I'm not thinking of marrying either a tiger or a gun, but a girl from the ranks of human beings. First you may draw up statistics of tiger populations in the different native states. Next you may investigate if there is a girl I can marry in the royal family of a state with a large tiger population." The dewan followed his orders. He found the right girl from a state which possessed a large number of tigers. Maharaja Jung Jung Bahadur killed five or six tigers each time he visited his father-in-law. In this manner, ninety-nine tiger skins adorned the walls of the reception hall in the Pratibandapuram palace.

V

The Maharaja's anxiety reached a fever pitch when there remained just one tiger to achieve his tally of a hundred. He had this one thought during the day and the same dream at night. By this time the tiger farms had run dry even in his father-in-law's kingdom. It became impossible to locate tigers anywhere. Yet

only one more was needed. If he could kill just that one single beast, the Maharaja would have no fears left. He could give up tiger hunting altogether. But he had to be extremely careful with that last tiger. What had the late chief astrologer said? "Even after killing ninety-nine tigers the Maharaja should beware of the hundredth..." True enough. The tiger was a savage beast after all. One had to be wary of it. But where was that hundredth tiger to be found? It seemed easier to find tiger's milk than a live tiger. Thus the Maharaja was sunk in gloom. But soon came the happy news which dispelled that gloom. In his own state sheep began to disappear frequently from a hillside village. It was first ascertained that this was not the work of Khader Mian Saheb or Virasami Naicker, both famed for their ability to swallow sheep whole. Surely, a tiger was at work. The villagers ran to inform the Maharaja. The Maharaja announced a three-year exemption from all taxes for that village and set out on the hunt at once. The tiger was not easily found. It seemed as if it had wantonly hid itself in order to flout the Maharaja's will. The Maharaja was equally determined. He refused to leave the forest until the tiger was found. As the days passed, the Maharaja's fury and obstinacy mounted alarmingly. Many officers lost their jobs. One day when his rage was at its height, the Maharaja called the dewan and ordered him to double the land tax forthwith "The people will become discontented. Then our state too will fall a prey to the Indian National Congress." "In that case you may resign from your post," said the king. The dewan went home convinced that if the Maharaja did not find the tiger soon, the results could be catastrophic.

He felt life returning to him only when he saw the tiger which had been brought from the People's Park in Madras and kept hidden in his house. At midnight when the town slept in peace, the dewan

and his aged wife dragged the tiger to the car and shoved it into the seat. The dewan himself drove the car straight to the forest where the Maharaja was hunting. When they reached the forest the tiger launched its satyagraha and refused to get out of the car. The dewan was thoroughly exhausted in his efforts to haul the beast out of the car and push it down to the ground. On the following day, the same old tiger wandered into the Maharaja's presence and stood as if in humble supplication, "Master, what do you command of me?" It was with boundless joy that the Maharaja took careful aim at the beast. The tiger fell in a crumpled heap. "I have killed the hundredth tiger. My vow has been fulfilled," the Maharaja was overcome with elation. Ordering the tiger to be brought to the capital in grand procession, the Maharaja hastened away in his car. After the Maharaja left, the hunters went to take a closer look at the tiger. The tiger looked back at them rolling its eyes in bafflement. The men realised that the tiger was not dead; the bullet had missed it. It had fainted from the shock of the bullet whizzing past. The hunters wondered what they should do. They decided that the Maharaja must not come to know that he had missed his target.

If he did, they could lose their jobs. One of the hunters took aim from a distance of one foot and shot the tiger. This time he killed it without missing his mark. Then, as commanded by the king, the dead tiger was taken in procession through the town and buried. A tomb was erected over it. A few days later the Maharaja's son's third birthday was celebrated. Until then the Maharaja had given his entire mind over to tiger hunting. He had had no time to spare for the crown prince. But now the king turned his attention to the child. He wished to give him some special gift on his birthday. He went to the shopping centre in Pratibandapuram and searched every shop, but couldn't find anything suitable. Finally he spotted a wooden tiger in a toyshop and decided it was the perfect gift. The wooden tiger cost only two annas and a quarter. But the shopkeeper knew that if he quoted such a low price to the Maharaja, he would be punished under the rules of the Emergency. So, he said, "Your Majesty, this is an extremely rare example of craftsmanship. A bargain at three hundred rupees!" "Very good. Let this be your offering to the crown prince on his birthday," said the king and took it away with him. On that day father and son played with that tiny little wooden tiger. It had been carved by an unskilled carpenter. Its surface was rough; tiny slivers of wood stood up like quills all over it. One of those slivers pierced the Maharaja's right hand. He pulled it out with his left hand and continued to play with the prince. The next day, infection flared in the Maharaja's right hand. In four days, it developed into a suppurating sore which spread all over the arm. Three famous surgeons were brought in from Madras. After holding a consultation they decided to operate. The operation took place. The three surgeons who performed it came out of the theatre and announced, "The operation was successful. The Maharaja is dead." In this manner the hundredth tiger took its final revenge upon the Tiger King.

CHAPTER EIGHT

The Enemy

Dr Sadao Hoki's house was built on a spot of the Japanese coast where as a little boy he had often played. The low, square stone house was set upon rocks well above a narrow beach that was outlined with bent pines. As a boy Sadao had climbed the pines, supporting himself on his bare feet, as he had seen men do in the South Seas when they climbed for coconuts.

His father had taken him often to the islands of those seas, and never had he failed to say to the little brave boy at his side, "Those islands yonder, they are the stepping stones to the future for Japan." "Where shall we step from them?" Sadao had asked seriously.

"Who knows?" his father had answered. "Who can limit our future? It depends on what we make it. Sadao had taken this into his mind as he did everything his father said, his father who never joked or played with him but who spent infinite pains upon him who was his only son. Sadao knew that his education was his father's chief concern.

For this reason he had been sent at twenty-two to America to learn all that could be learned of surgery and medicine. He had come back at thirty, and before his father died he had seen Sadao become famous not only as a surgeon but as a scientist. Because he was perfecting a discovery which would render wounds entirely clean, he had not been sent abroad with the troops. Also, he knew, there was some slight danger that the old General might need an operation for a condition for which he was now being treated medically, and for this possibility Sadao was being kept in Japan.

Clouds were rising from the ocean now. The unexpected warmth of the past few days had at night drawn heavy fog from the cold waves. Sadao watched mists hide outlines of a little island near the shore and then come creeping up the beach below the house, wreathing around the pines. In a few minutes fog would be wrapped about the house too. Then he would go into the room where Hana, his wife, would be waiting for him with the two children. But at this moment the door opened and she looked out, a dark-blue woollen haori1 over her kimono. She came to him affectionately and put her arm through his as he stood, smiled and said nothing. He had met Hana in America, but he had waited to fall in love with her until he was sure she was Japanese. His father would never have received her unless she had been pure in her race. He wondered often whom he would have married if he had not met Hana, and by what luck he had found her in the most casual way, by chance literally, at an American professor's house.

The professor and his wife had been kind people anxious to do something for their few foreign students, and the students, though bored, had accepted this kindness. Sadao had often told Hana how nearly he had not gone to Professor Harley's house that night — the rooms were so small, the food so bad, the professor's wife so voluble. But he had gone and there he had found Hana, a new student, and had felt he would love her if it were at all possible.

Now he felt her hand on his arm and was aware of the pleasure it gave him, even though they had been married years enough to have the two children. For they had not married heedlessly in America. They had finished their work at school and had come home to Japan, and when his father had seen her the marriage had been arranged in the old Japanese way, although Sadao and Hana had talked everything over beforehand. They were perfectly happy. She laid her cheek against his arm. It was at this moment that both of them saw something black come out of the mists. It was a man.

He was flung up out of the ocean — flung, it seemed, to his feet by a breaker. He staggered a few steps, his body outlined against the mist, his arms above his head. Then the curled mists hid him again. "Who is that?" Hana cried. She dropped Sadao's arm and they both leaned over the railing of the veranda. Now they saw him again.

The man was on his hands and knees crawling. Then they saw him fall on his face and lie there. "A fisherman perhaps," Sadao said, "washed from his boat." He ran quickly down the steps and behind him Hana came, her wide sleeves flying. A mile or two away on either side there were fishing villages, but here was only the bare and lonely coast, dangerous with rocks.

The surf beyond the beach was spiked with rocks. Somehow the man had managed to come through them — he must be badly torn. They saw when they came toward him that indeed it was so. The sand on one side of him had already a stain of red soaking through. "He is wounded," Sadao exclaimed. He made haste to the man, who lay motionless, his face in the sand. An old cap stuck to his head soaked with sea water. He was in wet rags of garments. Sadao stopped, Hana at his side, and turned the man's head. They saw the face. "A white man!" Hana whispered. Yes, it was a white man. The wet cap fell away and there was his wet yellow hair, long, as though for many weeks it had not been cut, and upon his young and tortured face was a rough yellow beard. He was unconscious and knew nothing that they did for him. Now Sadao remembered the wound, and with his expert fingers he began to search for it. Blood flowed freshly at his touch. On the right side of his lower back Sadao saw that a gun wound had been reopened. The flesh was blackened with powder. Sometime, not many days ago, the man had been shot and had not been tended. It was bad chance that the rock had struck the wound.

"Oh, how he is bleeding!" Hana whispered again in a solemn voice. The mists screened them now completely, and at this time of day no one came by. The fishermen had gone home and even the chance beachcombers would have considered the day at an end. "What shall we do with this man?" Sadao muttered. But his trained hands seemed of their own will to be doing what they could to stanch the fearful bleeding.

He packed the wound with the sea moss that strewed the beach. The man moaned with pain in his stupor but he did not awaken. "The best thing that we could do would be to put him back in the sea," Sadao said, answering himself. Now that the bleeding was stopped for the moment he stood up and dusted the sand from his hands. "Yes, undoubtedly that would be best," Hana said steadily. But she continued to stare down at the motionless man. "If we sheltered a white man in our house we should be arrested and if we turned him over as a prisoner, he would certainly die," Sadao said. "The kindest thing would be to put him back into the sea," Hana said. But neither of them moved.

They were staring with a curious repulsion upon the inert figure. "What is he?" Hana whispered. "There is something about him that looks American," Sadao said. He took up the battered cap. Yes, there, almost gone, was the faint lettering. "A sailor," he said, "from an American warship." He spelled it out: "U.S. Navy." The man was a prisoner of war! "He has escaped." Hana cried softly, "and that is why he is wounded." "In the back," Sadao agreed. They hesitated, looking at each other. Then Hana said with resolution: "Come, are we able to put him back into the sea?" "If I am able, are you?" Sadao asked. "No," Hana said, "But if you can do it alone..." Sadao hesitated again. "The strange thing is," he said, "that if the man were whole I could turn him over to the police without difficulty. I care nothing for him. He is my enemy. All Americans are my enemy. And he is only a common fellow. You see how foolish his face is. But since he is wounded..." "You also cannot throw him back to the sea," Hana said. "Then there is only one thing to do. We must carry him into the house." "But the servants?" Sadao inquired. "We must simply tell them that we intend to give him to the police — as indeed we must, Sadao. We must think of the children and your position. It would endanger all of us if we did not give this man over as a prisoner of war.

"Certainly," Sadao agreed. "I would not think of doing anything else." Thus agreed, together they lifted the man. He was very light, like a fowl that had been half-starved for a long time until it is only feathers and skeleton. So, his arms hanging, they carried him up the steps and into the side door of the house. This door opened into a passage, and down the passage they carried the man towards an empty bedroom. It had been the bedroom of Sadao's father, and since his death it had not been used. They laid the man on the deeply matted floor. Everything here had been Japanese to please the old man, who would never in his own home sit on a chair or sleep in a foreign bed. Hana went to the wall cupboards and slid back a door and took out a soft quilt.

She hesitated. The quilt was covered with flowered silk and the lining was pure white silk. "He is so dirty," she murmured in distress. "Yes, he had better be washed," Sadao agreed. "If you will fetch hot water I will wash him." "I cannot bear for you to touch him," she said. "We shall have to tell the servants he is here. I will tell Yumi now.

She can leave the children for a few minutes and she can wash him." Sadao considered a moment. "Let it be so," he agreed. "You tell Yumi and I will tell the others." But the utter pallor of the man's unconscious face moved him first to stoop and feel his pulse. It was faint but it was there. He put his hand against the man's cold breast. The heart too was yet alive. "He will die unless he is operated on," Sadao said, considering. "The question is whether he will not die anyway." Hana cried out in fear. "Don't try to save him! What if he should live?" "What if he should die?" Sadao replied. He stood gazing down on the motionless man. This man must have extraordinary vitality or he would have been dead by now. But then he was very young — perhaps not yet twentyfive. "You mean die from the operation?" Hana asked. "Yes," Sadao said.

Hana considered this doubtfully, and when she did not answer Sadao turned away. "At any rate something must be done with him," he said, "and first he must be washed." He went quickly out of the room and Hana came behind him. She did not wish to be left alone with the white man. He was the first she had seen since she left America and now he seemed to have nothing to do with those whom she had known there. Here he was her enemy, a menace, living or dead. She turned to the nursery and called, "Yumi!" But the children heard her voice and she had to go in for a moment and smile at them and play with the baby boy, now nearly three months old. Over the baby's soft black hair she motioned with her mouth, "Yumi — come with me!" "I will put the baby to bed," Yumi replied.

"He is ready." She went with Yumi into the bedroom next to the nursery and stood with the boy in her arms while Yumi spread the sleeping quilts on the floor and laid the baby between them. Then Hana led the way quickly and softly to the kitchen. The two servants were frightened at what their master had just told them. The old gardener, who was also a house servant, pulled the few hairs on his upper lip. "The master ought not to heal the wound of this white man," he said bluntly to Hana. "The white man ought to die. First he was shot. Then the sea caught him and wounded him with her rocks. If the master heals what the gun did and what the sea did they will take revenge on us." "I will tell him what you say," Hana replied courteously. But she herself was also frightened, although she was not superstitious as the old man was. Could it ever be well to help an enemy? Nevertheless she told Yumi to fetch the hot water and bring it to the room where the white man was. She went ahead and slid back the partitions. Sadao was not yet there. Yumi, following, put down her wooden bucket. Then she went over to the white man. When she saw him her thick lips folded themselves into stubbornness. "I have never washed a white man," she said, "and I will not wash so dirty a one now." Hana cried at her severely. "You will do what your master commands you!" There was so fierce a look of resistance upon Yumi's round dull face that Hana felt unreasonably afraid.

After all, if the servants should report something that was not as it happened? "Very well," she said with dignity. "You understand we only want to bring him to his senses so that we can turn him over as a prisoner?" "I will have nothing to do with it," Yumi said, "I am a poor person and it is not my business." "Then please," Hana said gently, "return to your own work." At once Yumi left the room. But this left Hana with the white man alone. She might have been too afraid to stay had not her anger at Yumi's stubbornness now sustained her. "Stupid Yumi," she muttered fiercely. "Is this anything but a man? And a wounded helpless man!" In the conviction of her own superiority she bent impulsively and untied the knotted rugs that kept the white man covered. When she had his breast bare she dipped the small clean towel that Yumi had brought into the steaming hot water and washed his face carefully. The man's skin, though rough with exposure, was of a fine texture and must have been very blond when he was a child. While she was thinking these thoughts, though not really liking the man better now that he was no longer a child, she kept on washing him until his upper body was quite clean. But she dared not turn him over. Where was Sadao? Now her anger was ebbing, and she was anxious again and she rose, wiping her hands on the wrong towel. Then lest the man be chilled, she put the quilt over him. "Sadao!" she called softly. He had been about to come in when she called. His hand had been on the door and now he opened it. She saw that he had brought his surgeon's emergency bag and that he wore his surgeon's coat. "You have decided to operate!" she cried. "Yes," he said shortly. He turned his back to her and unfolded a sterilized towel upon the floor of the tokonoma[2] alcove, and put his instruments out upon it. "Fetch towels," he said. She went obediently, but how anxious now, to the linen shelves and took out the towels. There ought also to be old pieces of matting so that the blood would not ruin the fine floor covering. She went out to the back veranda where the gardener kept strips of matting with which to protect delicate shrubs on cold nights and took an armful of them. But when she went back into the room, she saw this was useless. The blood had already soaked through the packing in the man's wound and had ruined the mat under him. "Oh, the mat!" she cried. "Yes, it is ruined," Sadao replied, as though he did not care. "Help me to turn him," he commanded her. She obeyed him without a word, and he began to wash the man's back carefully. "Yumi would not wash him," she said. "Did you wash him then?" Sadao asked, not stopping for a moment his swift concise movements. "Yes," she said. He did not seem to hear her. But she was used to his absorption when he was at work. She wondered for a moment if it mattered to him what was the body upon which he worked so long as it was for the work he did so excellently.

"You will have to give the anesthetic if he needs it," he said. "I?" she repeated blankly. "But never have I!" "It is easy enough," he said impatiently. He was taking out the packing now, and the blood began to flow more quickly. He peered into the wound with the bright surgeon's light fastened on his forehead. "The bullet is still there," he said with cool interest. "Now I wonder how deep this rock wound is. If it is not too deep it may be that I can get the bullet. But the bleeding is not superficial. He has lost much blood." At this moment Hana choked. He looked up and saw her face the colour of sulphur. "Don't faint," he said sharply. He did not put down his exploring instrument. "If I stop now the man will surely die." She clapped her hands to her mouth and leaped up and ran out of the room. Outside in the garden he heard her retching. But he went on with his work. "It will be better for her to empty her stomach," he thought. He had forgotten that of course she had never seen an operation. But her distress and his inability to go to her at once made him impatient and irritable with this man who lay like dead under his knife.

"This man." he thought, "there is no reason under heaven why he should live." Unconsciously this thought made him ruthless and he proceeded swiftly. In his dream the man moaned but Sadao paid no heed except to mutter at him. "Groan," he muttered, "groan if you like. I am not doing this for my own pleasure. In fact, I do not know why I am doing it." The door opened and there was Hana again.

"Where is the anesthetic?" she asked in a clear voice. Sadao motioned with his chin. "It is as well that you came back," he said. "This fellow is beginning to stir." She had the bottle and some cotton in her hand. "But how shall I do it?" she asked. "Simply saturate the cotton and hold it near his nostrils," Sadao replied without delaying for one moment the intricate detail of his work. "When he breathes badly move it away a little." She crouched close to the sleeping face of the young American. It was a piteously thin face, she thought, and the lips were twisted. The man was suffering whether he knew it or not.

Watching him, she wondered if the stories they heard sometimes of the sufferings of prisoners were true. They came like flickers of rumour, told by word of mouth and always contradicted. In the newspapers the reports were always that wherever the Japanese armies went the people received them gladly, with cries of joy at their liberation. But sometimes she remembered such men as General Takima, who at home beat his wife cruelly, though no one mentioned it now that he had fought so victorious a battle in Manchuria. If a man like that could be so cruel to a woman in his power, would he not be cruel to one like this for instance? She hoped anxiously that this young man had not been tortured. It was at this moment that she observed deep red scars on his neck, just under the ear. "Those scars," she murmured, lifting her eyes to Sadao. But he did not answer. At this moment he felt the tip of his instrument strike against something hard, dangerously near the kidney. All thought left him. He felt only the purest pleasure. He probed with his fingers, delicately, familiar with every atom of this human body. His old American professor of anatomy had seen to that knowledge. "Ignorance of the human body is the surgeon's cardinal sin, sirs!" he had thundered at his classes year after year. "To operate without as complete knowledge of the body as if you had made it — anything less than that is murder." "It is not quite at the kidney, my friend," Sadao murmured. It was his habit to murmur to the patient when he forgot himself in an operation. "My friend," he always called his patients and so now he did, forgetting that this was his enemy. Then quickly, with the cleanest and most precise of incisions, the bullet was out. The man quivered but he was still unconscious. Nevertheless he muttered a few English words. "Guts," he muttered, choking. "They got...my guts..." "Sadao!" Hana cried sharply. "Hush," Sadao said. The man sank again into silence so profound that Sadao took up his wrist, hating the touch of it. Yes, there was still a pulse so faint, so feeble, but enough, if he wanted the man to live, to give hope. "But certainly I do not want this man to live," he thought. "No more anesthetic," he told Hana. He turned as swiftly as though he had never paused and from his medicines he chose a small vial and from it filled a hypodermic and thrust it into the patient's left arm. Then putting down the needle, he took the man's wrist again. The pulse under his fingers fluttered once or twice and then grew stronger. "This man will live in spite of all," he said to Hana and sighed. The young man woke, so weak, his blue eyes so terrified when he perceived where he was, that Hana felt compelled to apologise. She herself served him, for none of the servants would enter the room. When she came in the first time, she saw him summon

his small strength to be prepared for some fearful thing. "Don't be afraid," she begged him softly. "How come... you speak English..." he gasped. "I was a long time in America," she replied.

She saw that he wanted to reply to that but he could not, and so she knelt and fed him gently from the porcelain spoon. He ate unwillingly, but still he ate. "Now you will soon be strong," she said, not liking him and yet moved to comfort him. He did not answer. When Sadao came in the third day after the operation, he found the young man sitting up, his face bloodless with the effort. "Lie down," Sadao cried. "Do you want to die?" He forced the man down gently and strongly and examined the wound. "You may kill yourself if you do this sort of thing," he scolded. "What are you going to do with me?" the boy muttered. He looked just now barely seventeen. "Are you going to hand me over?" For a moment Sadao did not answer. He finished his examination and then pulled the silk quilt over the man. "I do not know myself what I shall do with you," he said.

"I ought of course to give you to the police. You are a prisoner of war — no, do not tell me anything." He put up his hand as he saw the young man was about to speak. "Do not even tell me your name unless I ask it." They looked at each other for a moment, and then the young man closed his eyes and turned his face to the wall. "Okay," he whispered, his mouth a bitter line. Outside the door Hana was waiting for Sadao. He saw at once that she was in trouble. "Sadao, Yumi tells me the servants feel they cannot stay if we hide this man here any more," she said. "She tells me that they are saying that you and I were so long in America that we have forgotten to think of our own country first. They think we like Americans." "It is not true," Sadao said harshly "Americans are our enemies. But I have been trained not to let a man die if I can help it." "The servants cannot understand that," she said anxiously. "No," he agreed.

Neither seemed able to say more, and somehow the household dragged on. The servants grew more watchful. Their courtesy was as careful as ever, but their eyes were cold upon the pair to whom they were hired. "It is clear what our master ought to do," the old gardener said one morning. He had worked with flowers all his life, and had been a specialist too in moss. For Sadao's father he had made one of the finest moss gardens in Japan, sweeping the bright green carpet constantly so that not a leaf or a pine needle marred the velvet of its surface. "My old master's son knows very well what he ought to do," he now said, pinching a bud from a bush as he spoke. "When the man was so near death why did he not let him bleed?" "That young master is so proud of his skill to save life that he saves any life," the cook said contemptuously. She split a fowl's neck skillfully and held the fluttering bird and let its blood flow into the roots of a wistaria vine. Blood is the best of fertilisers, and the old gardener would not let her waste a drop of it. "It is the children of whom we must think," Yumi said sadly.

"What will be their fate if their father is condemned as a traitor?" They did not try to hide what they said from the ears of Hana as she stood arranging the day's flowers in the veranda near by, and she knew they spoke on purpose that she might hear. That they were right she knew too in most of her being. But there was another part of her which she herself could not understand.

It was not sentimental liking of the prisoner. She had come to think of him as a prisoner. She had not liked him even yesterday when he had said in his impulsive way, "Anyway, let me tell you that my name is Tom." She had only bowed her little distant bow. She saw hurt in his eyes but she did not wish to assuage it. Indeed, he was a great trouble in this house. As for Sadao, every day he examined the wound carefully. The last stitches had been pulled out this morning, and the young man would, in a fortnight be nearly as well as ever. Sadao went back to his office and carefully typed a letter to the Chief of police reporting the whole matter.

"On the twenty-first day of February an escaped prisoner was washed up on the shore in front of my house." So far he typed and then he opened a secret drawer of hisdesk and put the unfinished report into it. On the seventh day after that, two things happened. In the morning the servants left together, their belongings tied in large square cotton kerchiefs. When Hana got up in the morning nothing was done, the house not cleaned and the food not prepared, and she knew what it meant. She was dismayed and even terrified, but her pride as a mistress would not allow her to show it. Instead, she inclined her head gracefully when they appeared before her in the kitchen, and she paid them off and thanked them for all that they had done for her. They were crying, but she did not cry.

The cook and the gardener had served Sadao since he was a little boy in his father's house, and Yumi cried because of the children. She was so grieving that after she had gone she ran back to Hana. "If the baby misses me too much tonight, send for me. I am going to my own house and you know where it is." "Thank you," Hana said smiling. But she told herselfshe would not send for Yumi however the baby cried. She made the breakfast and Sadao helped with the children. Neither of them spoke of the servants beyond the fact that they were gone. But after Hana had taken morning food to the prisoner, she came back to Sadao. "Why is it we cannot see clearly what we ought to do?"

she asked him. "Even the servants see more clearly than we do. Why are we different from other Japanese?" Sadao did not answer. But a little later he went into the room where the prisoner was and said brusquely, "Today you may get up on your feet. I want you to stay up only five minutes at a time. Tomorrow you may try it twice as long. It would be well that you get back your strength as quickly as possible." He saw the flicker of terror on the young face that was still very pale. "Okay," the boy murmured. Evidently he was determined to say more. "I feel I ought to thank you, Doctor, for having saved my life." "Don't thank me too early," Sadao said coldly. He saw the flicker of terror again in the boy's eyes — terror as unmistakable as an animal's. The scars on his neck were crimson for a moment. Those scars! What were they?

Sadao did not ask. In the afternoon the second thing happened. Hana, working hard on unaccustomed labour, saw a messenger come to the door in official uniform. Her hands went weak and she could not draw her breath. The servants must have told already. She ran to Sadao, gasping, unable to utter a word. But by then the messenger had simply followed her through the garden and there he stood. She pointed at him helplessly. Sadao looked up from his book. He was in his office, the other partition of which was thrown open to the garden for the southern sunshine.

"What is it?" he asked the messenger and then he rose, seeing the man's uniform. "You are to come to the palace," the man said. "The old General is in pain again." "Oh," Hana breathed, "is that all?" "All?" the messenger exclaimed. "Is it not enough?"

"Indeed it is," she replied. "I am very sorry." When Sadao came to say goodbye, she was in the kitchen, but doing nothing. The children were asleep and she sat merely resting for a moment, more exhausted from her fright than from work "I thought they had come to arrest you", she said. He gazed down into her anxious eyes. "I must get rid of this man for your sake," he said in distress. "Somehow I must get rid of him." (Sadao goes to see the General) "Of course," the General said weakly, "I understand fully. But that is because, I once took a degree in Princeton. So few Japanese have." "I care nothing for the man, Excellency," Sadao said, "but having operated on him with such success..." "Yes, yes" the General said. "It only makes me feel you more indispensable to me.

Evidently you can save anyone — you are so skilled. You say you think I can stand one more such attack as I have had today?" "Not more than one," Sadao said. "Then certainly I can allow nothing to happen to you," the General said with anxiety. His long pale Japanese face became expressionless, which meant that he was in deep thought. "You cannot be arrested," the General said, closing his eyes. "Suppose you were condemned to death and the next day I had to have my operation?" "There are other surgeons, Excellency," Sadao suggested. "None I trust," the General replied.

"The best ones have been trained by Germans and would consider the operation successful even if I died. I do not care for their point of view." He sighed. "It seems a pity that we cannot better combine the German ruthlessness with the American sentimentality. Then you could turn your prisoner over to execution and yet I could be sure you would not murder me while I was unconscious." The General laughed. He had an unusual sense of humour. "As a Japanese, could you not combine these two foreign elements?" he asked. Sadao smiled. "I am not quite sure," he said, "but for your sake I would be willing to try, Excellency." The General shook his head.

"I had rather not be the test case," he said. He felt suddenly weak and overwhelmed with the cares of his life as an official in times such as these when repeated victory brought great responsibilities all over the south Pacific. "It is very unfortunate that this man should have washed up on your doorstep," he said irritably. "I feel it so myself," Sadao said gently. "It would be best if he could be quietly killed," the General said. "Not by you, but by someone who does not know him. I have my own private assassins. Suppose I send two of them to your house tonight or better, any night. You need know nothing about it. It is now warm — what would be more natural than that you should leave the outer partition of the white man's room open to the garden while he sleeps?"

"Certainly it would be very natural," Sadao agreed. "In fact, it is so left open every night." "Good," the General said, yawning. "They are very capable assassins — they make no noise and they know the trick of inward bleeding. If you like I can even have them remove the body." Sadao considered. "That perhaps would be best, Excellency," he agreed, thinking of Hana. He left the General's presence then and went home, thinking over the plan. In this way the whole thing would

be taken out of his hands. He would tell Hana nothing, since she would be timid at the idea of assassins in the house, and yet certainly such persons were essential in an absolute state such as Japan was. How else could rulers deal with those who opposed them? He refused to allow anything but reason to be the atmosphere of his mind as he went into the room where the American was in bed. But as he opened the door, to his surprise he found the young man out of bed, and preparing to go into the garden. "What is this!" he exclaimed. "Who gave you permission to leave your room?" "I'm not used to waiting for permission," Tom said gaily. "Gosh, I feel pretty good again! But will the muscles on this side always feel stiff?" "Is it so?" Sadao inquired, surprised. He forgot all else. "Now I thought I had provided against that," he murmured. He lifted the edge of the man's shirt and gazed at the healing scar. "Massage may do it," he said, "if exercise does not." "It won't bother me much," the young man said. His young face was gaunt under the stubbly blond beard. "Say, Doctor, I've got something I want to say to you. If I hadn't met a Jap like you — well, I wouldn't be alive today.

I know that." Sadao bowed but he could not speak. "Sure, I know that," Tom went on warmly. His big thin hands gripping a chair were white at the knuckles. "I guess if all the Japs were like you there wouldn't have been a war." "Perhaps," Sadao said with difficulty. "And now I think you had better go back to bed." He helped the boy back into bed and then bowed. "Good night," he said. Sadao slept badly that night. Time and time again he woke, thinking he heard the rustling of footsteps, the sound of a twig broken or a stone displaced in the garden — a noise such as men might make who carried a burden.

The next morning he made the excuse to go first into the guest room. If the American were gone he then could simply tell Hana that so the General had directed. But when he opened the door he saw at once that there on the pillow was the shaggy blond head. He could hear the peaceful breathing of sleep and he closed the door again quietly. "He is asleep," he told Hana.

"He is almost well to sleep like that." "What shall we do with him?" Hana whispered her old refrain. Sadao shook his head. "I must decide in a day or two," he promised. But certainly, he thought, the second night must be the night. There rose a wind that night, and he listened to the sounds of bending boughs and whistling partitions. Hana woke too. "Ought we not to go and close the sick man's partition?" she asked. "No," Sadao said. "He is able now to do it for himself." But the next morning the American was still there. Then the third night of course must be the night.

The wind changed to quiet rain and the garden was full of the sound of dripping eaves and running springs. Sadao slept a little better, but he woke at the sound of a crash and leaped to his feet. "What was that?" Hana cried. The baby woke at her voice and began to wail. "I must go and see," But he held her and would not let her move.

"Sadao," she cried, "what is the matter with you?" "Don't go," he muttered, "don't go!" His terror infected her and she stood breathless, waiting. There was only silence. Together they crept back into the bed, the baby between them. Yet when he opened the door of the guest room in the morning there was the young man. He was very gay and had already washed and was now on his feet. He had asked for a razor yesterday and had shaved himself and today there was a faint colour in his cheeks.

"I am well," he said joyously. Sadao drew his kimono round his weary body. He could not, he decided suddenly, go through another night. It was not that he cared for this young man's life. No, simply it was not worth the strain. "You are well," Sadao agreed. He lowered his voice. "You are so well that I think if I put my boat on the shore tonight, with food and extra clothing in it, you might be able to row to that little island not far from the coast. It is so near the coast that it has not been worth fortifying.

Nobody lives on it because in storm it is submerged. But this is not the season of storm. You could live there until you saw a Korean fishing boat pass by. They pass quite near the island because the water is many fathoms deep there." The young man stared at him, slowly omprehending. "Do I have to?" he asked. "I think so," Sadao said gently. "You unerstand — it is not hidden that you are here. The young man nodded in perfect comprehension. "Okay," he said simply. Sadao did not see him again until evening.

As soon as it was dark he had dragged the stout boat down to the shore and in it he put food and bottled water that he had bought secretly during the day, as well as two quilts he had bought at a pawnshop. The boat he tied to a post in the water, for the tide was high. There was no moon and he worked without a flashlight. When he came to the house he entered as though he were just back from his work, and so Hana knew nothing. "Yumi was here today," she said as she served his supper. Though she was so modern, still she did not eat with him. "Yumi cried over the baby," she went on with a sigh. "She misses him so." "The servants will come back as soon as the foreigner is gone," Sadao said. He went into the guest room that night before he went to bed himself and checked carefully the American's temperature, the state of the wound, and his heart and pulse. The pulse was irregular but that was perhaps because of excitement. The young man's pale lips were pressed together and his eyes burned. Only the scars on his neck were red. "I realise you are saving my life again," he told Sadao. "Not at all," Sadao said. "It is only inconvenient to have you here any longer." He had hesitated a good deal about giving the man a flashlight. But he had decided to give it to him after all. It was a small one, his own, which he used at night when he was called.

"If your food runs out before you catch a boat," he said, "signal me two flashes at the same instant the sun drops over the horizon. Do not signal in darkness, for it will be seen. If you are all right but still there, signal me once. You will find fresh fish easy to catch but you must eat them raw. A fire would be seen." "Okay," the young man breathed. He was dressed now in the Japanese clothes which Sadao had given him, and at the last moment Sadao wrapped a black cloth about his blond head.

"Now," Sadao said. The young American, without a word, shook Sadao's hand warmly, and then walked quite well across the floor and down the step into the darkness of the garden. Once — twice... Sadao saw his light flash to find his way. But that would not be suspected. He waited until from the shore there was one more flash. Then he closed the partition. That night he slept. "You say the man escaped?" the General asked faintly. He had been operated upon a week before, an emergency operation to which Sadao had been called in the night. For twelve hours Sadao had not been sure the General would live.

The gall bladder was much involved. Then the old man had begun to breathe deeply again and to demand food. Sadao had not been able to ask about the assassins. So far as he knew they had never come. The servants had returned and Yumi had cleaned the guest room thoroughly and had burned sulphur in it to get the white man's smell out of it. Nobody said anything.

Only the gardener was cross because he had got behind with his chrysanthemums. But after a week Sadao felt the General was well enough to be spoken to about the prisoner. "Yes, Excellency, he escaped," Sadao now said. He coughed, signifying that he had not said all he might have said, but was unwilling to disturb the General further. But the old man opened his eyes suddenly. "That prisoner," he said with some energy, "did I not promise you I would kill him for you?" "You did, Excellency," Sadao said. "Well, well!" the old man said in a tone of amazement, "so I did! But you see, I was suffering a good deal. The truth is, I thought of nothing but myself.

In short, I forgot my promise to you." "I wondered, Your Excellency," Sadao murmured. "It was certainly very careless of me," the General said. "But you understand it was not lack of patriotism or dereliction of duty." He looked anxiously at his doctor. "If the matter should come out you would understand that, wouldn't you?" "Certainly, Your Excellency," Sadao said. He suddenly comprehended that the General was in the palm of his hand and that as a consequence he himself was perfectly safe.

"I can swear to your loyalty, Excellency," he said to the old General, "and to your zeal against the enemy." "You are a good man," the General murmured and closed his eyes." "You will be rewarded." But Sadao, searching the spot of black in the twilighted sea that night, had his reward. There was no prick of light in the dusk. No one was on the island. His prisoner was gone — safe, doubtless, for he had warned him to wait only for a Korean fishing boat. He stood for a moment on the veranda, gazing out to the sea from whence the young man had come that other night. And into his mind, although without reason, there came other white faces he had known — the professor at whose house he had met Hana, a dull man, and his wife had been a silly talkative woman, in spite of her wish to be kind. He remembered his old teacher of anatomy, who had been so insistent on mercy with the knife, and then he remembered the face of his fat and slatternly landlady. He had had great difficulty in finding a place to live in America because he was a Japanese. The Americans were full of prejudice and it had been bitter to live in it, knowing himselftheir superior.

How he had despised the ignorant and dirty old woman who had at last consented to house him in her miserable home! He had once tried to be grateful to her because she had in his last year nursed him through influenza, but it was difficult, for she was no less repulsive to him in her kindness. Now he remembered the youthful, haggard face of his prisoner — white and repulsive. "Strange," he thought. "I wonder why I could not kill him?

HighlightNoteWeb Search

CHAPTER NINE

On the face of it

Derry had a burnt face. He avoided people and liked secluded places. He jumped over a wall to enter Mr. Lamb's garden because he thought it was empty. He was startled when Mr. Lamb 'spoke to him.Derry suffers from a sense of inferiority complex. He has a burnt face People find his face very terrible. So he wants to avoid them. So he is not afraid of them but people afraid of him.Derry is a teenager who has a burnt face. This makes him lonely and withdrawn. He avoids men and their company. He comes to Mr. Lamb's garden in search of loneliness. The meeting with Mr. Lamb is a meeting of two minds with totally opposite views. Derry is withdrawn and Mr. Lamb is very social. Mr. Lamb is always ready to welcome anyone who enters his garden. Mr. Lamb has a tin leg. One of his legs was blown off in the war. Children tease him by calling 'Lamey Lamb'. But he doesn't mind it Mr. Lamb is satisfied with the life that God has granted. He is always cheerful and tries to comfort others.

Mr. Lamb thought that fire had burnt Derry's face. But Derry told him that it was acid that burnt his face. He feels that people are afraid of him. It has left a deep scaron his mind too. According to Derry, people were afraid of his burnt face. Derry thought that no one would ever kiss him except his mother. When people startled, he felt they were afraid of him. Derry thought that people considered him as a 'devil'.Mr. Lamb has a tin leg. One of his legs was blown off in the war. He uses an artificial tin leg for walking. But Mr. Lamb doesn't feel himself a crippled person. The children tell him Lamey Lamb but he does not mind it. There was a man who was afraid of every thing. A bus might run over him. A donkey might kick him to death. So he went into his room. He locked the door. A picture fell off the wall on to his head and killed him. Mr. Lamb doesn't want Derry to alienate himself. Mr. Lamb's disability could not stop him going outside. He hates to live behind the curtains. He likes to live in open. He talks to the children who come to his garden. He enjoys people's talks. He suggests Derry not to be alienated from the main stream. Mr. Lamb says that alienation or withdrawal is not the solution of the problem Derry wants to live isolate from people. For him people are not just. But Mr. Lamb lives among the people. He keeps his heart always open to them. They are not so as Derry thanks. The following qualities of Mr. Lamb attracted Derry towards him. First, he inspires Derry to face the world. Second, he advises Derry to stop crying on what people say about his face. Third, he is always cheerful and tries to comfort others. Mr. Lamb gives the example of a flower' and 'a weed'. He tells that a wood is also a green growing plant as is a flower. So, there is no diffrence between a weed and a flower. A weed is also as important as a flower. Mr. Lamb says that once Derry gets home, he will never let himself come back again. But Derry says that he will come back. Mr. Lamb should wait for him. Dey comes back. His mother tries her best to hold him back. Derry's mother should have heard many things about Mr. Lamb. People warned her. Therefore she asks Derry not to go to Mr. Lamb. Derry asks her mother not to believe all that she hears. He is determined to go there. Derry can't stay to help Mr. Lamb to get crab-apples because he has been away from home for long. His mother must be worried. He is fourteen but his mother still wants to know where her son is now. These words are a mirror to the way Mr. Lamb thinks and behaves. He has a positive attitude towards life. Both the nature as well as human life attract him the same way. His interest in the things keeps him busy and away from negative feelings.

Mr. Lamb has a garden. There are plants of apples, pears and he grows weeds and flower in his garden. He sits in his garden and talk to those who come in to the garden.Mr. Lamb was picking ripe crab apples. He was alone there. He fell from the ladder and died. When Derry reached there he found him dead. He began to weep. He was so late that he couldn't help him. Mr. Lamb is an old man. He lives alone in a big house. He has a garden. He is very social. He is always ready to welcome anyone who enters his garden. He has lost his one leg in the war. He uses a tin leg. Children tease him by calling 'Lamey Lamb'. But he doesn't mind it. He is satisfied with the life God has granted. He is always cheerful. He tries to comfort others. He inspires Derry, the very withdrawn and defiant boy, to face the world and love life. He advises Derry to stop crying on what people say about his face. He says that a weed is also as important as a flower. Thus Mr. Lamb is a good human being. The play On The Face Of It' features an old man and a small boy. The man is Mr. Lamb and the boy Derry who meets him in Mr. Lamb's garden. Derry is withdrawn and defiant. He does not like being with people.

Mr. Lamb's meeting with Derry brings a turning point in Derry's life. He gives confidence to Derry. He persuades him that he can get better than rest of the people. He should stop hating people. Hatred burns oneself away inside. Derry should take life as it is. This leaves a deep impression on Derry. He comes back to Mr. Lamb only to find him dead. But Mr. Lamb brings a change in Derry's life. He develops confidence to face the world in a more positive way.

memories of Childhood

1. The Cutting Of My Long Hair

Zitkala-Sa found her new place having bitter cold. There was snow on the ground. The trees were bare. Harsh noises of the ringing of the bell and the clatter of the shoes annoyed her sensitive cars. Her spirit tore itself in struggling for its lost freedom. Zitkala-Sa was placed in a line of girls who were marching into the dining room. These were Indian girls. They were in stiff shoes and closely clinging dresses. Small girls wore sleeved aprons and shingled hair. Zitkala-Sa disappeared unnoticed. She came to a large room with three white beds in it. She crawled under the bed and hid herself in the dark corner. She couldn't hide herself for long. They searched her into the room and dragged her out. When the first bell rang all pupils pulled out their chairs from under the table. Zitkala-Sa also pulled out her chair and sat on it. But she saw no one was seated so she stood up. When second bell rang all girls sat and began to eat. But Zitkala-Sa did not sit and began to feel uncomfortable. Zitkala-Sa had long and beautiful hair. In her culture the long and beautiful hair of coward was cut short. She was not coward. According to her culture Zitkala-Sa opposed to cut her hair . Zitkala-Sa was alone. Her mother was not there to console her. Her hair was cut. People stared at her. She tossed like a doll. She moaned in auguish. She was like an animal driven by a herd man. Late in the morning, Zitkala-Sa's friend Judewin gave her a terrible warning. Judewin knew a few words of English, and she had overheard the pale face woman talk about cutting their long heavy hair. Zitkala-Sa was carried downstairs and tied fast in a chair. She cried aloud shaking her head all the while until she felt the cold blades of the scissors against her neck, and heard them gnaw one of her thick braids. The narrator's friend Judewin gave her a terrible warning. She had over heard the pale face woman. She talked about cutting the long and heavy hair of Indian girls. The narrator had made a decision. She was not to submit, she was to struggle and fight against that oppression. The narrator disappeared unnoticed. She crawled under the bed and cuddled her self in the dark corner. She shuddered with fear whenever she heard foot steps nearby. Voices became louder. They stormed into the room. She was dragged out. She resisted by kicking and scratching wildly. She was carried downstairs and tied fast in a chair. Then they gnawed off her long and beautiful hair. No one came forward to help her. Nor was any body present there to console her.

Thus, the narrator lost her distinct cultural recognition and identity.

2. We Too Are Human Beings

Bama took about half an hour to an hour to cover the distance from her chool to home. She used to watch all the fun, and games on the way and all the entertaining novelties and oddities in the street, the shops and the bazar. The narrator stood at her street. Just then an elder man of her street came from the bazar. He was carrying a small packet. He was holding the packet by its string without touching it. Seeing this, she was doubled up with laughter. Bama felt that the elderly man's behaviour was funny because he was carrying a small packet of food by its string without touching it thought he was a big man. She thought it quite funny. Bama's elder brother told her why the elder carried the packet with a string They were not allowed to touch the things which the upper caste used. This made her terribly sad and provoked. Bama was highly inspired by the words of her elder brother. There was only ne hope for the people of her caste. They could attain dignity and honour if they were kamned. Bama studied very hard and stood first in her class. The title 'We Too Are Human Beings' is appropriate. The so-called untouch able are too human beings in all similarity as are the so-called upper caste people. Social inequality and untouchability must be abolished. Annan offered advice of studying with care, learning all she can, to be ahead in her lessons and to work hard. Then the people will come to her and attach themselves to her.

Zitkala-Sa was an American Indian. The white people wanted American Indians to adopt their culture. Zitkala-Sa rebelled against the cruel way in which Indian girls were forced to have short hair and dress like them. Her hair was cut short. She was powerless. But her spirit could not suppressed.

Bama was born in a low caste family in India. The upper caste people discrimi nated against the low caste people. They could not touch the food of upper class Untouchability is a curse for low caste in India. Bama's spirit revolted against this injustice. She could not understand why they were considered untouchable. She wanted that they should be understood respectable and human beings.

CHAPTER ELEVEN

My Mother at Sixty-Six

Stanza – 1

My Mother at Sixty-Six:
Driving from my parent's
home to Cochin last Friday
morning, I saw my mother,
beside me,
doze, open mouthed, her face
ashen like that
of a corpse

Reference – These well-known eye-catching lines have been adopted from the poem – "My Mother at Sixty-Six", written by a very prominent Poet – "Kamala Das", a leading Indo-Anglian poet.

Context – The time when the poet approaches Cochin airport with her mother, she sadly realizes looking at her mother's wrinkled face that the old age was reflecting on her mother's face.

Explanation – Early morning, it was Friday when the poet departure for Cochin airport driving car with her mother. Poet's mother was sitting just beside her in the car. She looked at her mother, who was dozing, open mouthed there. She realized that her mother's face was lifeless and devoid of colour, pale face. It seemed as if she were dead. This scene was quite anguishing to the poet.

Stanza – 2

and realized with pain
that she was as old as she
looked but soon
put that thought away, and
looked out at Young
Trees sprinting, the merry children spilling

out of their homes,

Reference – These well-known eye-catching lines have been adopted from the poem – "My Mother at Sixty-Six", written by a very prominent Poet – "Kamala Das", a leading Indo-Anglian poet.

Context – In these lines, seeing on her mother's face, the poet realized that her face now reflected older age. It was quite unbearable to her and to shift her attention from that painful scene, she diverted her attention seeing out-side of the car at the delighted sights.

Explanation – It was an anguishing sight for the poet to behold her mother's old age face. Now, when it became unbearable for her, she diverted her thoughts away, she glanced out of the car. Somewhere these scenes of life and energy were giving her pleasure; lightened her heart. Sprinting young trees and running children out of their houses merrily would also make her feel delighted and pleasure some.

Stanza – 3

.... but after the airport's
security check, standing a few yards
away, I looked again at her, wan, pale
as a late winter's moon and felt that old
familiar ache, my childhood's fear,
but all I said was, see you soon, Amma,
all I did was smile and smile and
smile......

Reference – These well-known eye-catching lines have been adopted from the poem – "My Mother at Sixty-Six", written by a very prominent Poet – "Kamala Das", a leading Indo-Anglian poet.

Context – Now, the poet is at the airport, once again the same fear of losing her mother came to her but she pretends to put away her fears away and bids her goodbye with a smile.

Explanation – Having passed through the security check at the airport, the poet looks at her mother from a few yards away. Once again, she looked at her mother's face which seemed as a yellowish and dull like the moon of the late winter that filled her heart with her childhood pain. It was the fear of losing her mother. It was quite painful and anxious; therefore, she could only say to her mother, "See you soon, Amma." At that time, she was hiding her pain from her mother. She only smiles and smiles and smiles and bade her goodbye.

Important – Late winter's moon – The moon – in the last phase of winter lacks its normal glow. The poet's mother too lacks strength and glow of her face. The poet, therefore, compares her to the late winter's moon.

Difficult words -

1) doze: a short, light sleep

2) ashen: very pale, like ash.

3) corpse: a dead body.

4) sprinting: here, shooting out of the ground.

5) spilling: here, to move out in great numbers.

6) wan: unnaturally pale, as from physical or emotional distress.

7) ache: pain.

1. Simile: It is the comparison of two things by using as or like.

Exp - "her face ashen like that of a corpse", "as a late winter's moon".

2. Metaphor: it is the direct comparison of two things without the use of as or like.

Exp - "the merry children spilling".

3. Personification: When we give human characteristics to animals or plants or non-living things. e.g., "trees sprinting".

4. Anaphora: It is the repetition of a word or phrase to create a poetic effect in a poem.

e.g., the poet repeats these words, "smile and smile and smile".

5. Alliteration: It is the repetition of the consonant sounds in a line of a poem.

e.g., "my mother", "that thought", "I said was, see you soon".

CHAPTER TWELVE

An Elementary School Classroom In A Slum

Stanza -1

Far far from gusty waves these children's faces.
Like rootless weeds, the hair torn round their pallor:
The tall girl with her weighed-down head. The paper
Seeming boy, with rat's eyes.

Reference – These well-known eye-catching lines have been adopted from the poem – "An Elementary School Classroom in a Slum", written by a very prominent Poet – "Stephen Spender".

Context –In these lines the poet describes the sorrowful state of children in a school of slum. He talks about a boy and a girl and their pathetic as well as helpless condition that these children experience so early in their life.

Explanation -The slum school children are far away from the hope of bright and hopeful life of the rich world outside. These children have no hope on their faces. Their faces are unkempt and dirty. Their hairs are scattered untidily around their pale faces. The children appear like rootless weeds The tall girl who is sitting there is depressed due to the burden of poverty and keeps her head down. The boy who is sitting there is very thin and his eyes are bulging out like that of the rat (implying hungry eyes).

Stanza -2

The stunted, unlucky heir
Of twisted bones, reciting a father's gnarled disease,
His lesson from his desk.
At back of the dim class
One unnoted, sweet and young. His eyes live in a dream,
Of squirrel's game, in the tree room, other than this.

Reference –These well-known eye-catching lines have been adopted from the poem – "An Elementary School Classroom in a Slum", written by a very prominent Poet – "Stephen Spender".

Context –Here, in these lines' poet describes the two children's physical and mental abnormalities who belong to slum school.

Explanation -Here, the poet seems to describe the physical growth of the boy who seems to have blocked and his body appears under-developed. He is an unfortunate heir who has inherited the twisted bones of his father. Actually, he is not reciting a lesson from his desk. He is enumerating the disease inherited from his father. An innocent young boy sits at the back of the dim class. He is unnoticed. Dreams seem to be alive in his eyes. He dreams of outdoor games, outside his dull classroom in a dirty slum. He dreams of squirrel playing games in the hollow space of the tree. His dreams are of the places other than his repulsive classroom (Young boy lost in the world of his dreams. He creates his own fantastic world where he plays like a squirrel in her tree room. The dull & monotonous environment of the classroom does not interest him).

Stanza –3

> On sour cream walls, donations, Shakespeare's head,
> Cloudless at dawn, civilized dome riding all cities.
> Belled, flowery, Tyrolese valley. Open-handed map
> Awarding the world its world.

Reference –These well-known eye-catching lines have been adopted from the poem – "An Elementary School Classroom in a Slum", written by a very prominent Poet – "Stephen Spender".

Context – In these lines, the poet describes the decoration on the walls of the classroom, which Show pictures of another unknown world.

Explanation – The colour painted on the wall is an unpleasant cream colour which was done by donations. The gifts given as donations and the picture of Shakespeare are hung on the unpleasant creamy walls (reflecting despondency). But they are useless. Shakespeare and literature are no good to them. The other things are also hung on the classroom walls like the picture of a clear sky at dawn and a beautiful Tyrolese valley (indicating beauty and hope with its bells and flowers) along with a dome of an ancient city building standing for civilization and progress (the rich people pretend to be generous by donating these things to the children, they feel they have gifted them the beautiful world through these donations).

Stanza –4

And yet, for these Children, these windows,
Not this map, their world, Where all their future's painted with a fog,
A narrow street sealed in with a lead sky
Far far from rivers, capes, and stars of words.

Reference –These well-known eye-catching lines have been adopted from the poem – "An Elementary School Classroom in a Slum", written by a very prominent Poet – "Stephen Spender".

Context –The poet says a contrast between the world outside and the world of the slum children who sit within a dreary room in dreary surroundings.

Explanation -The poet says that for the slum children, their limited world is what they can see through the windows of the classroom. Their future is foggy, bleak and dull. Their life/world is confined within the narrow streets of the slum enclosed by the bluish grey sky. Their world is far from rivers, seas that indicate adventure and beautiful world, they are also far away from stars which symbolizes wisdom that can empower their future.

Stanza –5

Surely, Shakespeare is wicked, the map a bad example,
With ships and sun and love tempting them to steal
For lives that slyly turn in their cramped holes
From fog to endless night? On their slag heap, these children
Wear skins peeped through by bones and spectacles of steel
With mended glass, like bottle bits on stones.
All of their time and space are foggy slum
So, blot their maps with slums as big as doom.

Reference –These well-known eye-catching lines have been adopted from the poem – "An Elementary School Classroom in a Slum", written by a very prominent Poet – "Stephen Spender".

Context – Here in these lines, the poet wants to prove meaninglessness and unsuitability of the pictures and the map hanging on the walls of the slum school's classroom.

Explanation –Here, Shakespeare is described as wicked as he holds the key to charmed world of letters and unfortunately for these children, there is no way that they can enter that world and the map is bad example for them as it does not hold any place for these slum children. They are cruel temptations for the slum children. These poor innocent children long to have adventure (ships), a better life (sun) and love, as they are depicted on the classroom walls. These children's lives are confined to the narrow holes (dark slums) that they are living in and their lives secretly turn around in their pitiable state. They only have uncertainty (fog) and hopelessness (endless night) with themselves. The poet has compared their emaciated wasted bodies to slag (waste) heaped together, their bones peep out of their flesh (because of malnourishment). These children wear steel spectacles with cracked glasses looking like repaired pieces of a glass-bottle lying on stones (suggesting immense poverty). All their time and space are confined to the uncertain world of slums. These slums are living hells and they are a blot on the progress of the rich and civilized world.

Stanza -6

Unless, governor, inspector, visitor,
This map becomes their window and these windows
That shut upon their lives like catacombs,
Break O break open till they break the town
And show the children green fields, and make their world
Run azure on gold sands, and let their tongues
Run naked into books the white and green leaves open
History theirs whose language is the sun.

Reference –These well-known eye-catching lines have been adopted from the poem – "An Elementary School Classroom in a Slum", written by a very prominent Poet – "Stephen Spender".

Context –The poet is trying to suggest the measures which the administration should take to improve the lot of the slum children and bring change in their lives.

Explanation –Here, the poet describes the dilemma of the slum area saying that there is no coordination between the map of the civilized world and the world of the children. Governors, teachers, inspectors and visitors must abridge this gap. They must peep into the world of the children living in slums and make their world the world of the children too. Their unsuitable environment of the slums has shut all their gates of progress. Their slums are like the internal dark part of graves. He uses the words „Break O break open" to say that they have to break out from the miserable hopeless life of the slum world so that they can wander beyond the slums and their town on to the green fields. These obstacles should be broken.

Everything that binds them should be broken and they must be allowed to breathe in the open air. Let them come out of their narrow lanes and dirty slums of the town. Their world should extend to the sky-blue & waves rising over the golden sands (indicating the unlimited world). Let the pages of wisdom be open for them. They should also be provided with the opportunity to learn lessons from nature. Let their tongue run freely without any check or fear (they must taste all joys of life). Only those people make or create history whose language has the warmth and strength of the sun (people whose language has the touch of humanity, those who have the true knowledge and through this they can break the chains of prevailing norms, can create history. The poets wants „like" opportunities to be made available to these children). These deprived children must be taught to express themselves freely. He wishes that all distinctions of the rich and the poor and all forms of injustice should be wiped out so that no childhood gets lost in the gloomy darkness and ignorance in the slums.

<u>Figures of speech in the poem</u>

 <u>Simile</u>
 Like rootless weeds
 <u>Metaphor</u>
 The paperseeming boy
 <u>Metaphor</u>
 Civilized dome riding all cities
 <u>Metaphor</u>
 Their future's painted with a fog
 <u>Metaphor</u>
 A narrow street sealed in with a lead sky
 <u>Metaphor</u>
 Lives that slyly turn in their cramped holes
 <u>Metaphor</u>
 On their slag heap
 <u>Simile</u>
 Like bottle bits on stones
 <u>Simile</u>
 These windows That shut upon their lives like catacombs
 <u>Metaphor</u>
 History is theirs whose language is the sun

CHAPTER THIRTEEN

Keeping Quiet (Pablo Neruda)

Stanza - 1

"Now we will count to twelve
and we will all keep still.
For once on the face of the Earth
let's not speak in any language,
let's stop for one second,
and not move our arms so much."

Reference – These well-known eye-catching lines have been adopted from the poem – "Keeping Quiet", written by a very prominent Poet – "Pablo Neruda".

Context – In these lines, the poet is talking about keeping still and quiet till he counts to twelve. It'll be an exotic moment when all will be together in a strange situation.

Explanation - The poet here requests everyone to count till twelve in their own mind and to stop for a while. May be this 'twelve' referred by the poet is the twelve hours in the clock or the twelve months in a year. He wants everyone to stop and calm down. The poet urges everyone not to speak any language. As we all know that there are different languages spoken in different parts of the earth which sometimes become a barrier in our way for peace. So, he asks people not to speak. Not only this, but he also wants us to stop moving our arms. By using the word 'arms' he means the weapons which are used by different countries to raise a war against each other. So basically, the poet is demanding peace from all of us.

Stanza - 2

"It would be an exotic moment
without rush, without engines,
we would all be together
in a sudden strangeness. Fishermen in the cold sea

would not harm whales
and the man gathering salt
would look at his hurt hands."

Reference – These well-known eye-catching lines have been adopted from the poem – "Keeping Quiet", written by a very prominent Poet – "Pablo Neruda".

Context – Here, the poet request all the men who are performing their tasks to keep quiet and still till he finishes counting to twelve.

Explanation - Poet says that it would be a rare situation when there will be no engines working. Here he wants to stay that if everything comes to standstill, it will be a very different moment. If all the engines like the vehicles and machines stop, then there will be a sudden, strange situation as the world will experience a sudden calmness. People will not be in a rush to achieve material things one after another. Further, the poet says that the fisherman will also stop and not harm whales in the sea. This means that the poet is urging everyone not to harm the animals. Here he gives the example of whales which are being hunted for the purpose of food or trade. He also wants people to calm down so that they can stop and see what they have achieved or lost. For this, he gives the example of the man who gathers salt, whose hands are hurt. Here he wants everyone to stop for a while in order to see and feel their achievements and how much they have lost for the sake of attaining such materialistic things.

Stanza – 3

Those who prepare green wars,
wars with gas, wars with fire,
victory with no survivors,
would put on clean clothes
and walk about with their brothers in the shade, doing nothing.
What I want should not be confused with total inactivity.
Life is what it is about; I want no truck with death.

Reference – These well-known eye-catching lines have been adopted from the poem – "Keeping Quiet", written by a very prominent Poet – "Pablo Neruda".

Context - In these lines the poet describes the importance of keeping quiet and still for some moments during our daily activities. Doing so will provide us an opportunity to introspect, revaluate our actions and redetermine our future plans for the better.

Explanation - The poet asks everyone to stop those activities which are damaging the environment. Today all human beings are making money by damaging the environment with their activities such as mining, deforestation, letting the chemical waste into rivers, etc. The poet asks us not to do so. He also requests people not to involve in wars as there is no benefit of achieving such victory in which no one is left alive. He says so because wars and environmental damage will lead to no life on earth. Rather, he wants people to adopt a new approach towards life and mankind. He says that you should treat your enemy like brothers and promote peace and harmony in the world.

Stanza – 4

If we were not so single-minded
about keeping our lives moving,
and for once could nothing
perhaps a huge silence
might interrupt this sadness
of never understanding ourselves
and of threatening ourselves with death.

Reference – These well-known eye-catching lines have been adopted from the poem – "Keeping Quiet", written by a very prominent Poet – "Pablo Neruda".

Context –The poet here talks about man's ceaseless efforts and complete involvement in merely pulling on with their lives. He does not pause once and tries to understand the greater meaning of life.

Explanation –Now the poet wants to clarify to his readers that when he asks them to stop from saying or doing anything, he doesn't want anyone to become a non-active person. Non-active is a person who remains idle and doesn't do anything. Here, he simply means that we should stop and see the consequences of our deeds. The poet doesn't want to see people being killed due to their greed for money and the expansion of territories. Further, he says that people are continuously working to achieve their tasks without even thinking about their results. They are in fear of death and therefore, want to achieve most of the things before their death. Here he urges them to stop for a while and take some moment to relish what they have achieved till now. Everyone here is living a life in which he wants to achieve various things one after another. But now the poet says it is the time to stop and see what has been achieved and should be enjoyed. This will help us skip the sadness which has become so prominent in our lives. The sadness of not enjoying what we have achieved and the greed to achieve what next is on the list to be achieved.

Stanza – 5

Perhaps the Earth can teach us
as when everything seems dead
and later proves to be alive.
Now I'll count up to twelve
and you keep quiet and I will go.

Reference – These well-known eye-catching lines have been adopted from the poem – "Keeping Quiet", written by a very prominent Poet – "Pablo Neruda".

Context – Insisting upon the need for keeping quiet for a moment and doing nothing, the poet exhorts us to learn from the earth which seems dead in autumn but becomes full of life in spring.

Explanation - In these lines, the poet suggests to human beings that we should learn a lesson from Earth. During the winters everything freezes and becomes lifeless. But when the season changes and it's the onset of the spring season, everything presents in nature such as the trees, birds, rivers, etc. gets life. So here, the poet, by giving the example of nature, wants to say that all human beings should stop and try to judge their deeds. They can try and make their life better with calmness, peace. Finally, he ends up by saying that now he will count up to twelve so that we all may become quiet. Here 'quiet' means to calm down ourselves and move towards the path of peace and harmony. After saying this he says 'I will go'. He says so as he has conveyed his message to the people and wants them to be left alone to think about it and work in the direction of peace.

Literary devices: -

Assonance: Use of vowel sound 'o' and 'e'
- (Now we will count to twelve, not move our arms so much)

Anaphora: Two consecutive lines starting with the word 'Let's'
- Let's not speak in any language, let's stop for one second,

Alliteration: the repetition of a consonant sound at the start of two or more closely placed words.
- 'We will' – 'w' sound is repeated

Alliteration: 'we would' – 'w' sound is repeated, 'sudden strangeness' – 's' sound is repeated, 'his hurt hands' – 'h' sound is repeated

Alliteration: 'wars with' – 'w' sound is repeated, 'clean clothes' – 'c' sound is repeated

Assonance: use of vowel 'o' (victory with no survivors, would put on clean clothes and walk about with their brothers)

Repetition: use of 'war'

Alliteration: we were, so single-minded

Enjambment: and for once could perhaps a huge silence....... of threatening ourselves with death.

A thing of Beauty

A thing of Beauty (John Keats)

<u>Stanza – 1</u>

A thing of beauty is a joy forever

Its loveliness increases, it will never

Pass into nothingness, but will keep

A bower quiet for us, and a sleep

Full of sweet dreams, and health, and quiet breathing.

Reference – These well-known eye-catching lines have been adopted from the poem – "A Thing of Beauty", written by a very prominent Poet – "John Keats".

Context – In these lines, the poet praises the beautiful things for their profound and joyous effect that they provide us.

Reference - The poet says that a thing of beauty is permanent which stays forever. It never fades away. Rather, it increases with the passing time. It is a source of endless joy for us. It provides us with a shelter full of quietude, a sleep with sweet dreams and health with soft breathing. For the poet, beauty is like a beautiful shady tree under whose shade all the creatures can sleep peacefully and enjoy good health.

Bower: A shady place under the tree

<u>Literary devices:</u>

Rhyme scheme: aabbc (forever, never, keep, sleep, breathing)

<u>**Alliteration:**</u> Use of consonant sound at the start of two words which are close in series (Sleep-Sweet)

<u>**Metaphor:**</u> bower Quiet (calmness of the bower is compared to the calming effect of a beautiful thing)

<u>Stanza – 2</u>

Therefore, on every morrow, are we wreathing

A flowery band to bind us to the earth,

Spite of despondence, of the inhuman dearth
Of noble natures, of the gloomy days,
Of all the unhealthy and o'er-darkened ways
Made for our searching: yes, in spite of all,
Some shape of beauty moves away the pall
From our dark spirits.

Reference – These well-known eye-catching lines have been adopted from the poem – "A Thing of Beauty", written by a very prominent Poet – "John Keats".

Context – In these lines, Keats describes the beautiful things that are the sources of immense of joy for us. It has a number of blessings to give us such as a quiet shelter, a sleep with sweet dreams and health with quiet breathing.

Explanation - The poet says that every day, it is the beauty which fills us with the spirit to live. It is the beauty which builds the desire in us to live though there are sad moments and cruel people around us. So here the poet wants to say that without beauty the earth will be full of cruel people, sad and gloomy moments. It is the beauty which is created by God which helps us to remove the sadness from our hearts.

Stanza – 3

Such the sun, the moon,
Trees old, and young, sprouting a shady boon
For simple sheep; and such are daffodils
With the green world they live in; and clear rills
That for themselves a cooling covert make
'Gainst the hot season; the mid forest brake.
Rich with a sprinkling of fair musk-rose blooms.

Reference – These well-known eye-catching lines have been adopted from the poem – "A Thing of Beauty", written by a very prominent Poet – "John Keats".

Context –Here the poet celebrates the soothing beauty of nature in the wilderness; Pristine and colourful in its glory.

Explanation – Here in these lines, the poet describes the beautiful things which are present on earth such as the sun, moon, trees, flowers (daffodils) and the rivers. The poet says that all these things are like a blessing bestowed on all the creatures by earth. He further describes that the trees provide us with their shade, flowers with their beauty and rivers with their coolness during the hot summers. Then there is a thick mass of ferns in the middle of the forest that bear sweet smelling musk-roses. All of these are the beauties of nature which are like a boon for us.

Literary devices:

Alliteration: Use of consonant sound at the start of two words which are close in series ('s' in Sprouting Shady, Simple sheep, 'c' in cooling covert)

Imagery: Trees giving shade (sprouting shady boon), growing process of daffodils (daffodils with the green world they live in), Clean River streams (Clear rills)

Antithesis: opposite words placed together (old and young)

Stanza – 4

And such too is the grandeur of the dooms
We have imagined for the mighty dead;
All lovely tales that we have heard or read;
An endless fountain of immortal drink,
Pouring unto us from the heaven's brink.

Reference – These well-known eye-catching lines have been adopted from the poem – "A Thing of Beauty", written by a very prominent Poet – "John Keats".

Context – In these lines, after describing the beauty of nature, the poet now describes the things of beauty made by human hands.

Explanation – The poet says that he also admires the fertile imagination of those builders and architects of the bygone era, who built the beautiful domes to adorn the mausoleums of great and powerful people who changed and made history. Then he describes the tales of the mighty warriors who laid their lives for their countries or for humanity. He says that these beautiful things are the gifts from God for all of us. They are like a nectar given by god to us and these are those beauties which are immortal and give us a reason to live on this earth despite having so many sorrows in our life.

Literary devices:

Alliteration: Use of consonant sound at the start of two words which are close in series ('h' in have heard)

Metaphor: Immortal drinks (beautiful objects of nature are forever like a never-ending portion of a drink)

Rhyme: Rhyme scheme is used in every stanza of the poem (forever; never, keep; sleep, dead; read etc.)

Imagery: Bushes full of musk roses (sprinkling of fair musk rose blooms), books describing valour of fighters (grandeur-..mighty dead), god providing us with best things (pouring from the heaven's brink)